Lone Star Ladies

A Travel Guide to Women's History in Texas

Melinda Rice

Republic of Texas Press
Plano, Texas

Library of Congress Cataloging-in-Publication Data

Rice, Melinda.
   Lone Star ladies: a travel guide to women's history in Texas. / Melinda Rice.
      p. cm.
   Includes bibliographical references (p.) and index.
   ISBN 1-55622-847-3 (pbk.)
   1. Women--Texas--History. 2. Historic sites--Texas--Guidebooks.
   3. Texas--Guidebooks. I. Title.

   HQ1438.T4 R53   2001
   305.4'09764--dc21   2001041902
                                                              CIP

© 2002, Melinda Rice

All Rights Reserved

Printed in the United States of America

ISBN 1-55622-847-3
10 9 8 7 6 5 4 3 2 1
0109

All inquiries for volume purchases of this book should be addressed to
Wordware Publishing, Inc., at 2320 Los Rios Boulevard, Plano, Texas
75074. Telephone inquiries may be made by calling:

(972) 423-0090

For Katherine and Ninni, Babe and Bonnie,
Hallie and all the other women in these pages.

Contents

Acknowledgments. xi
Introduction xiii
Author's Note. xv

People and Their Places

Women of the Alamo. 2
   The Alamo 2
   Susanna Dickinson Hannig Sites. 4
      The Lives of Susanna Dickinson Hannig
      and Angelina Dickinson Griffith 6
   Clara Driscoll Site 9
      The Lives of Adina De Zavala and Clara
      Driscoll, and the Daughters of the Republic
      of Texas 11
   More Alamo Biographies 15
      Ana Salazar Esparza and María de Jesús
      Castro Esparza. 15
      Juana Navarro Alsbury and
      Gertrudis Navarro. 16
      Concepción Losoya and Juana
      Francisca Melton 19
      Victoriana de Salinas and her daughters 20
Common Law and an Uncommon Woman. 21
   Harriet Ames Site. 21
      The Life of Harriet Ames 21
Moms Turned Moguls 25
   Mary Kay Ash Site 25
      The Life of Mary Kay Ash. 26
   Nina Baird Sites. 28
      Fort Worth Plant. 28

Contents

Abilene Plant. 29
Lubbock Plant 29
Waco Plant 30
The Life of Nina Baird. 30
The Circus Queen of the Southwest. 33
Mollie Bailey Site 33
The Life of Mollie Bailey 34
Capital Women 37
The Texas State Capitol 37
Miriam Ferguson Sites 39
The Life of Miriam "Ma" Ferguson. 40
Minnie Fisher Cunningham Sites 42
The Life of Minnie Fisher Cunningham 43
Barbara Jordan Sites 47
The Life of Barbara Jordan 47
Annie Blanton Site 50
The Life of Annie Webb Blanton 50
From Half Time to the Big Time 52
Gussie Nell Davis and Rangerette Site 52
The Life of Gussie Nell Davis and the
Kilgore College Rangerettes 53
Panhandle Mystery Woman 57
Frenchy McCormick Sites 57
The Life of Frenchy McCormick 58
Bird Lady of Texas 62
Connie Hagar Sites 62
The Life of Connie Hagar 65
Pioneer and Town Founder 67
Margaret Hallett Sites 67
The Life of Margaret Hallett 68
Teacher, Rancher, and Chili Cook-off Queen 72
Hallie Stillwell Site 72
The Life of Hallie Stillwell 73
Ladies of Letters 77
Dilue Rose Harris Site 77

The Life of Dilue Rose Harris. 78
Katherine Anne Porter Sites 79
    The Life of Katherine Anne Porter 81
Sarah McClendon Site 83
    The Life of Sarah McClendon. 84
Sallie Reynolds Matthews Site 85
    The Life of Sallie Reynolds Matthews 86
The Musically Inclined 88
Olga Samaroff Site. 88
    The Life of Olga Samaroff 88
Janis Joplin Site 91
    The Life of Janis Joplin 91
Selena Sites 94
    The Life of Selena Quintanilla Perez 97
Artful Daubers. 101
Elizabet Ney Sites 101
    The Life of Elizabet Ney 102
Georgia O'Keeffe Sites 104
    The Life of Georgia O'Keeffe 106
The Ultimate Philanthropist 109
Ima Hogg Sites. 109
    The Life of Ima Hogg. 112
Medicine Women 115
May Owen Site. 115
    The Life of May Owen 115
Frances "Daisy" Allen Site 117
    The Life of Frances Allen 118
Texas's Yellow Rose 120
Myth or Heroine of the Revolution? 120
The Yellow Rose of Texas Site 120
    The Legend of the Yellow Rose of Texas 120
Ladies of the Links 124
Babe Didrikson Zaharias Sites 124
    The Life of Babe Didrikson Zaharias 126
Betsy Rawls Site. 129

The Life of Betsy Rawls 130
A Reformer in Bloom 131
   Claudia Alta "Lady Bird" Taylor Johnson Sites . . . 131
      The Life of Lady Bird Johnson. 134
From Texas to Temperance 138
   Carry Nation Site 138
      The Life of Carry Nation. 138
West Texas Woman 140
   Annie Riggs Site 140
      The Life of Annie Riggs 142
Sanctified and Vilified 143
   Martha White McWhirter Sites 143
      The Life of Martha White McWhirter and
      the Sanctificationists 144
Indian Captives 148
   Cynthia Ann Parker, Rachel Parker Plummer,
   and Elizabeth Kellogg Site. 148
      The Life of Rachel Parker Plummer. 149
      The Life of Cynthia Ann Parker 150
Doyenne of a Ranching Dynasty 154
   Henrietta King Sites. 154
      The Life of Henrietta King. 154
The Mother of Texas 157
   Jane Long Sites. 157
      The Life of Jane Wilkinson Long 157
Texas Bad Girl. 160
   Bonnie Parker Sites 160
      The Life of Bonnie Parker 161
Fly Girls 166
   Bessie Coleman Site. 166
      The Life of Bessie Coleman 167
   The Stinson Sisters Site. 170
      The Lives of the Stinson Sisters. 171
   Women Airforce Service Pilots Sites 174
      The Life of the Women Airforce
      Service Pilots. 180

Other Places and Their People

Jefferson, Texas 186
    Diamond Bessie 189
Johnson Space Center. 192
    Sally Ride. 193
    Mae Jemison 194
    Ellen Ochoa 196
    Shannon Lucid 198
    Eileen Collins 200
Miss Hattie's Bordello Museum 203
Museum of the Gulf Coast 204
National Cowgirl Hall of Fame 206
Texas Black Woman's Archives 207
Texas Woman's University 208
The Women's Museum: An Institute for the Future . . . 211

Suggested Itineraries 213
    Day Trips: 213
        In and Around Dallas/Fort Worth 213
        In and Around Houston 215
        In and Around Austin. 216
        In San Antonio 217
    Multi-day Trips: 217
        Northeast Texas 217
        East Texas 219
        Southeast Texas 220
        South Texas 221
        The Hill Country 222
        West Texas 222
        The Panhandle 224

Index 225
Photo Index 231

Acknowledgments

Lone Star Ladies: A Travel Guide to Women's History in Texas never would have made it from the "Gee, this is a good idea" phase to your hands without the help of many people—librarians, historians, researchers, history buffs, the friends and family who keep me (relatively) sane.

In particular, I want to thank:

Chris Floerke and Tom Shelton at the Institute of Texan Cultures for their thorough, cheerful help tracking down photographs;

Margaret and Douglas Hoke for their gracious hospitality, their enthusiasm for this project, and their devotion to the memory of Miss Ima Hogg;

Varner-Hogg State Historical Park's Jeff Hutchinson;

Jefferson resident Marcia Thomas;

Ginnie Bivona at Republic of Texas Press;

Doug Wintermute, PIO extraordinaire at Kilgore College;

The fabulous staff of the Woman's Collection at Texas Woman's University;

Michael Grauer, curator of art at the Amarillo Museum of Art;

John Neal Phillips, for helping me wade through the myths surrounding Bonnie Parker;

Lisa Struthers of the San Jacinto Museum of History Association;

All the helpful folks at the Babe Didrikson Zaharias Museum;

LeAnna Biles and Jackie Johnson at the Annie Riggs Memorial Museum;

Kacy Carraway at NASA;

The phenomenal staff of the Lena Armstrong Public Library in Belton;

Ian McGuire at the Bell County Museum;

Darcy Johnson and Mike Pacino at Cal Farley's Boys Ranch;

Dadie Stillwell Potter;

Anna Peebler at the Rosenberg Public Library in Galveston;

Ellen Brown of The Texas Collection at Baylor University;

Thanks also to Joy Dickinson, Nancy Schaadt, Lin Tripicco, Tod Casasent, and Virginia Whitehill for their support and encouragement; my nieces Bethany and Katherine Dicken and their brother Davis, who never once admonished me for missing their school events and birthday parties because I was off working on this book; and the rest of my family for just putting up with me during the research and writing process.

And finally, thanks to David Rice: friend, supporter, photographer, inspiration, ginger tea-maker, and all-around great husband.

Introduction

There is properly no history, only biography.
—Ralph Waldo Emerson

... women have a special contribution to make to any
group enterprise, and I feel it is up to them to contribute
the kinds of awareness that relatively few men... have
incorporated through their education.
—Margaret Mead

Why?

That is the most common question asked about this book. Why write a travel guide to women's history in Texas?

Well, to mangle George Leigh Mallory (who replied "Because it is there" when asked why he wanted to climb Mount Everest): because it *isn't* there.

If you want to hike, bike, shop, sail, camp, or scuba dive... see flowers, art, amphibians, rocks, or old forts... sample barbecue, hangover cures, or mineral baths in Texas—there's a guidebook for you.

But until now there was no comprehensive guide to Texas sites commemorating women's achievements and contributions to history. Flip through this book. I guarantee you will discover a woman or place heretofore unknown to you.

Since this is a travel book, many notable women are not mentioned simply because there is no specific place in Texas associated with them to visit. You won't find chapters on WAC Commander Oveta Culp Hobby, prolific nineteenth-century writer Amelia Barr, or celebrated bad girl Belle Starr.

You *will* find, among others, the Women Airforce Service Pilots and their predecessors the Stinson sisters, artist

Elizabet Ney, golfer Babe Didrikson Zaharias, rancher and all-purpose character Hallie Stillwell, and that *other* celebrated bad girl, Bonnie Parker. There are artists, authors, and athletes; politicians, reformers, and healers, and characters of all kinds.

If you visit every site listed in this book, you will travel from the bayous and piney woods of East Texas to the dusty plains of the West; from the Panhandle to the Gulf of Mexico.

Whether you hop in the car to take a tour or stick strictly to armchair travel, have a nice trip. You're bound to meet some interesting people along the way.

Author's Note

Every effort has been made to ensure the information in this book is accurate. But phone numbers, hours of operation, and Internet addresses do change, so it is best to verify before visiting. As of press time, all contact information was correct. Please let me know if you discover something that should be updated, or if there is a site that should be included in future editions of *Lone Star Ladies*. P.O. Box 202588, Arlington, Texas 76006.

People and Their Places

· Women of the Alamo ·

The names most readily associated with the Alamo belong to the Y-chromosome set—Jim Bowie, William Travis, Davy Crockett, Santa Anna. But the little mission-turned-fort in San Antonio brims with tales of women, too. Some were noncombatants during the siege that made the Alamo famous in 1836 during Texas's rebellion against Mexico. **Susanna Dickinson Hannig** and her daughter **Angelina**, **Victoriana de Salinas** and her three daughters along with **Ana Salazar Esparza**, **Juana Navarro Alsbury**, **Gertrudis Navarro**, **Maria de Jesus Castro Esparza**, **Concepción Losoya**, **Juana Francisca Melton**, and **Petra Gonzales** survived that battle. One woman, an anonymous African American who was most likely a slave, did not. Survivors reported she was killed while trying to cross the Alamo grounds, and her body was found sprawled between two cannon.

Seven decades later **Adina De Zavala** and **Clara Driscoll** rallied the Daughters of the Republic of Texas and fought to preserve the Alamo when businessmen wanted to tear down the mission and redevelop the property.

Today the Alamo is a monument to all these women—the one who died, the ones delivered from the siege there, and those who delivered it to posterity. It bridges gaps across culture and time to make them, forever, the Women of the Alamo.

The Alamo

Don't be fooled by all the strategically shot photos that make the **Alamo** look like the Little Mission on the Prairie. It's smack in the middle of downtown San Antonio, a block or so from the Riverwalk and a shopping mall. To get there, take I-35

The Alamo

Photo courtesy of the San Antonio Convention and Visitor's Bureau

to San Antonio. Take the exit toward I-37 and watch for Commerce Street. Exit onto Commerce Street, then turn right onto Alamo Plaza. The Alamo complex is about two blocks on the right, across the street from a shady little city park.

Plan your visit for first thing in the morning or on Sundays to avoid the crowds. "Avoid" is a relative term since the Alamo attracts more than 2.5 million visitors each year. Set your expectations accordingly. The Long Barracks, in particular, can be a trial for the claustrophobic.

The chapel and the Long Barracks Museum are the only buildings remaining from the original mission complex. The outer walls and buildings that house the library and gift shop were added during restoration.

Don't miss the **Long Barracks Museum.** It includes a small display about siege survivors and a larger one about the fight to save and preserve the Alamo as a state historic site. A bronze plaque affixed to the outside of the building hails Clara Driscoll for bankrolling the preservation project.

Hours: 9 A.M. to 5:30 P.M. Mon.-Sat.
   10 A.M. to 5:30 P.M. Sundays
Admission: Free
Location: Alamo Plaza in downtown San Antonio, between
   E. Houston and E. Crockett streets, two blocks from
   Rivercenter Mall.
Phone Number: 210-225-1391
Fax: 210-229-1343
Mailing Address: P.O. Box 2599, San Antonio, Texas
   78299
Web Address: www.thealamo.org

Daughters of the Republic of Texas Library, which is part of the Alamo complex, has specific information about the women who were its survivors and saviors. This is not a lending library. Access is restricted to researchers. Call for an appointment.

Hours: 9 A.M. to 5 P.M., Mon.-Sat.
Phone Number: 210-225-1071
Fax: 210-212-8514
Mailing Address: P.O. Box 1401, San Antonio, Texas
   78295-1401
Web Address: www.drtl.org

Susanna Dickinson Hannig Sites

In **Lockhart** (about 30 minutes from Austin) there is a **historical marker** at 308 W. San Antonio Street, two blocks off the town square. Susanna lived with her fifth husband in a house

Susanna A. Dickinson

Photo courtesy of the UT Institute of Texan Cultures at San Antonio

that used to be on the site, which is now occupied by Lockhart's city hall.

In **Austin**, a building at **501 W. Fifth Street** (where it intersects with Neches Street) used to be Susanna's home. Most recently a barbecue joint, the vacant building has been the subject of a fierce debate about whether to preserve it. In March of 2001 the Austin City Council voted to spend more than half a million dollars to have it moved to a city-owned lot on the northwest corner of Tenth Street and Congress Avenue.

The move should be completed by the end of 2001. The building eventually will be restored, outfitted as a museum, and opened to the public.

Susanna is buried in **Oakwood Cemetery**, 1601 Navasota Street, in Austin.

The Lives of Susanna Dickinson Hannig and Angelina Dickinson Griffith

During her lifetime, Susanna was both hailed as a heroine and condemned as a harlot. She was a daughter, mother, and grandmother, and a wife to five different husbands. She survived the siege of the Alamo and was mother to "the Babe of the Alamo." She was one of the first women to divorce in Harris County. By the time she died, she was a Texas legend.

She started life as Susanna Wilkerson (sometimes given as Wilkinson) in rural Tennessee, probably in 1814. Fifteen years later, on May 24, 1829, she married Almeron Dickinson.

According to one family story, Susanna quarreled with Almeron when they were still courting. The couple broke up and Almeron soon became engaged to one of Susanna's friends. The friend planned a wedding with none other than Susanna as a bridesmaid—a plan thwarted when Susanna eloped with Almeron herself.

The couple was living near Gonzales, Texas, by early 1831, and their daughter, Angelina Elizabeth, was born on December 14, 1834.

Susanna and her child stayed in Gonzales when Almeron went off to fight in San Antonio the following year, but they joined him within months. Volunteers rallying to the Texas cause had looted the Dickinson home, terrorizing Susanna in the process and wounding a local doctor who defended her.

The Dickinson family retreated behind the walls of the Alamo when Santa Anna and his troops arrived in San Antonio on February 23, 1836. Legend has it that William Travis gave his cat's-eye ring to Angelina, threading it onto a string and tying it around the baby's neck himself.

Throughout the thirteen-day siege, Susanna helped nurse the sick and wounded.

Mother and child were captured when the Alamo fell on March 6. According to family accounts, she told a historian, "The struggle had lasted more than two hours when my husband rushed into the church where I was with my child, and exclaimed: 'Great God, Sue, the Mexicans are inside our walls! All is lost! If they spare you, save my child!' Then, with a parting kiss, he drew his sword and plunged into the strife then raging in different portions of the fortification."

It is unlikely the uneducated, unsophisticated Susanna would have used such florid phrasing, but this account of her last meeting with Almeron can be found in many sources. It has been repeated so often that is has become part of the Alamo folklore.

Santa Anna interviewed Susanna along with the other noncombatants and reportedly offered to adopt Angelina. When Susanna refused, he gave mother and child a blanket, two dollars in silver, and a message to deliver to Sam Houston who was commanding the Texas troops.

She delivered it, bringing word of the Alamo's fall to the world and earning a small degree of fame for herself in the process. She was proclaimed a heroine in newspaper accounts, and Angelina was dubbed "the Babe of the Alamo."

But they could not live on tales of glory. Susanna needed a way to support herself and Angelina. When she applied to the newly formed Texas government for $500, her fame did her little good and the request was denied.

Illiterate and without family or resources, she moved to Houston and finally decided to marry again. She began living with a man named John Williams and married him in November of 1837. But Williams was abusive, and according to some accounts he beat Susanna and Angelina. Less than four months after the marriage, Susanna became one of the first people in Harris County to get a divorce.

She tried matrimony again, marrying Francis Herring on December 20, 1838. He died in 1843, leaving her once again a widow. But this time she was not without resources. By 1839 the state had granted the heirs of Almeron Dickinson the rights to 640 acres of land—not in consideration for their losses, but for the military service rendered by Almeron.

Between her third and fourth marriages, Susanna lived—at least for a time—in the Mansion House Hotel, a known brothel operated by the infamous Pamelia Mann, who at various times was charged with forgery, assault, larceny, and "fornication." Long before the Chicken Ranch made headlines, Ms. Mann and her girls were raising...um...eyebrows and tarnishing reputations in Harris County.

Susanna tried matrimony again in 1847 with a Pennsylvanian named Peter Bellis—an experiment that failed within seven years. This time it was the husband who filed for divorce, claiming Susanna left him to live in a "house of ill fame"—the Mansion House Hotel—and accusing her of adultery and prostitution. Never mind that according to some accounts, Bellis met his future ex-wife in that very same brothel.

Despite her notoriety in Houston, a local minister praised Susanna during this time for nursing cholera victims. She joined his congregation and he baptized her in Buffalo Bayou in 1849, but family accounts say the gossip of other members eventually drove her from the church.

In 1855, shortly after Susanna's second divorce and Angelina's first marriage, mother and daughter were awarded an additional 1,920 acres of land thanks to Almeron and the Alamo.

Angelina had married a farmer many years her senior on June 8, 1851, in Houston. Family accounts say Susanna handpicked John Maynard Griffith for her strong-willed and often disobedient daughter.

The "Babe of the Alamo" gave birth to three children in six years—Almeron Dickinson Griffith in 1853, Susanna Griffith in 1855, and Joseph Griffith in 1857—but she was unhappy. Angelina divorced her husband and headed for New Orleans, leaving her oldest child with an uncle and the two youngest in a convent, but taking with her a reputation for wild ways and promiscuity.

She eventually married again and had another child, Sallie, in 1865. When Angelina died four years later, reportedly of a uterine hemorrhage, she was living in Galveston and working as a prostitute. She was thirty-four years old.

Susanna and her fifth husband took in all four grandchildren. In 1857 she had married Joseph William Hannig in Lockhart. They soon moved to Austin, taking the grandchildren with them. Hannig became a successful furniture maker there, and Susanna became a respected member of society.

In the 1870s she told a journalist she had "lost her reason" for a time after the fall of the Alamo.

Susanna died on October 7, 1883, after a six-month illness. Hannig remarried but he was buried beside Susanna when he died seven years later.

Clara Driscoll Site

In 1914 Clara gave her twelve-acre estate, **Laguna Gloria**, to the Texas Fine Arts Association to be used "as a museum to bring pleasure in the appreciation of art to the people of Texas." The Austin Museum of Art, which now owns the property, recently announced a major renovation of the site that includes the house Clara lived in and an art school. The house is currently closed for renovations, but the art school is open and the grounds are available for rental.

Clara Driscoll as a young woman

Photo courtesy of the UT Institute of Texan Cultures at San Antonio

Hours: 10 A.M. to 5 P.M. Tues.-Wed. and Fri.-Sat.
10 A.M. to 8 P.M. Thursdays
Noon to 5 P.M. Sundays
Closed Mondays
Admission: Free
Location: Austin, about 12 miles from the airport, on a bluff overlooking Lake Austin. From the airport, take Hwy. 71 west to Riverside Drive and turn right. Follow Riverside to Lamar Boulevard and turn right. Head north to 6th Street and turn left, staying in the right lane until it splits. Take the right fork onto the ramp to access Loop 1 (Mopac) North. Exit at 35th Street. Turn left and stay on 35th until it dead ends at the entrance to the grounds.
Phone number: 512-495-9224
Fax: 512-454-9408
Address: 3809 W. 35th Street, Austin, Texas 78703
Web Address: www.amoa.org

The Lives of Adina De Zavala and Clara Driscoll, and the Daughters of the Republic of Texas

All the combatants in the 1836 siege of the Alamo were men, but the second battle of the Alamo was initiated and carried out by women. Though they started out on the same side in the war to preserve the Alamo, Adina and Clara became implacable enemies and ended up battling each other.

As the granddaughter of Texas hero Lorenzo De Zavala, Adina grew up acutely aware of her Texas heritage. She was born November 28, 1861, in Harris County, the first of Augustine and Julia De Zavala's six children. She attended Ursuline Academy in Galveston until 1873, when she rejoined her parents and siblings, who had moved to San Antonio. She later attended Sam Houston Normal Institute and a music school in Missouri. Adina returned to Texas as a teacher, working first in Terrell then in San Antonio.

In 1889 she organized a group of women who gathered to discuss Texas history and its preservation. This group joined with the new Daughters of the Republic of Texas in 1893, forming the De Zavala Chapter of that group.

Clara, too, grew up imbued with Texas history. Both her grandfathers fought in the Texas Revolution. She was born on April 2, 1881, in St. Mary's, Texas, the only daughter of Robert and Julia Driscoll. By the time she was ten, her father was a multimillionaire thanks to investments in banking, ranching, and other businesses.

As a result, Clara attended private schools in Texas, New York City, and France. She returned to Texas in about 1899 and joined the De Zavala Chapter of the DRT.

By that time the organization was operating the Alamo chapel, which had been purchased by the state of Texas in 1893. But the rest of the property, including the Long Barracks where much of the most vicious fighting had occurred, belonged to a wholesale grocery firm called Hugo and Schmeltzer Company. Adina had a verbal promise from the owners that the DRT would have first option if the grocers decided to sell the property.

When she found out an Eastern hotel syndicate had offered $75,000 for the site—and was near to purchasing the property—she mobilized the DRT to scrounge money to buy it. But they simply could not raise enough fast enough.

Enter Clara Driscoll and her bank account. First Clara paid money to extend the DRT's option on the site, then she finally took on the debt herself and bought the property in order to save it. In 1905 the DRT and the state bought the property from Clara—with the state contributing $65,000 of the $75,000 and the DRT supplying the other $10,000.

But that was the easy part compared to what was coming. The second battle of the Alamo split the DRT between Adina's supporters and Clara's.

Adina wanted to preserve as much of the existing stonework as possible, while Clara wanted to raze much of the

Portrait of Adina De Zavala, 1900s.
This picture was published on the cover of sheet music for
"Remember the Alamo," by Jessie Beattie Thomas, 1908.
Photo courtesy of the UT Institute of Texan Cultures at San Antonio

property in the mistaken belief that only the chapel had been built before the 1836 Alamo siege.

The battle was fought in the courts, the newspapers, and in public opinion. At one point in 1908, Adina even barricaded herself inside the property's north barrack for three days to protest its destruction.

But finally even Adina's status as a member of DRT's state executive committee couldn't help her. She lost the fight, and control went to Clara and her supporters.

Adina left the DRT and founded The Daughters and Sons of the Heroes and Pioneers of the Republic of Texas, and the Texas Historical Landmarks Society. In 1923 she was appointed to the Texas Historical Board by the governor, and in the 1930s she helped plan the celebrations for the Texas Centennial. She wrote about Texas history and belonged to many organizations dedicated to helping women: the Texas Woman's Press Association, the San Antonio Women's League for Betterment of the Life of Women, the Women's Club, and the Woman's Parliament.

Adina died on March 1, 1955. Time and some diligent historical research proved she had been right about the age and historical significance of many Alamo sites.

Clara, dubbed the "Savior of the Alamo" in the press, moved to New York City during the court battles over the mission complex. She wrote books and plays, including a collection of short stories called *In the Shadow of the Alamo*.

In 1906 she married Henry Hulme Sevier, a newspaperman and former Texas legislator, at St. Patrick's Cathedral in New York City. They lived in Long Island, and Clara was president of the Texas Club there.

The couple moved to Austin in 1914 when Clara's father died. While there, Clara served as president of the DRT. The couple moved again in 1929, this time to Palo Alto. A woman ahead of her time, Clara became president of the Corpus Christi Bank and Trust Company upon the death of her brother.

Under her leadership its value nearly doubled. In 1933 she moved to Chile with her husband, who had been appointed U.S. ambassador there.

But in 1935 she returned to Texas and separated from her husband. Still a woman ahead of her time, she resumed her maiden name when they divorced. It would be another forty years or so before that practice became widespread and socially acceptable.

Like Adina, Clara helped plan the celebrations for the Texas Centennial, worked with the Federation of Women's Clubs, and continued her preservation work. Unlike Adina, she got into politics.

Clara was a longtime national committeewoman for the Democratic Party and worked behind the scenes to elect John Nance Garner and Franklin Roosevelt. She was as good at politics as she was at business, and political candidates curried her favor.

She died unexpectedly in 1945 of a cerebral hemorrhage. After lying in state in the Alamo chapel, she was buried in the Masonic Cemetery in San Antonio.

More Alamo Biographies

Ana Salazar Esparza and María de Jesús Castro Esparza

Ana and Maria, like Susanna and Angelina, were a mother and daughter who survived the Alamo siege. But their post-Alamo lives were much less colorful.

Little is known of Ana's early life. She married Victor de Castro and was left alone to raise their daughter, Maria, when he died.

Ana's second husband, Gregorio, was one of many Mexicans who fought for Texas during its struggle for independence from Mexico. He had planned to evacuate his family from San

Antonio, but Mexican troops prevented that with their arrival on February 23, 1836. So he took Ana, Maria, and their three sons to the Alamo for protection. The gates were already barred, but they managed to get in through a chapel window.

Ana and her children were taken prisoner thirteen days later after Mexican troops (Ana's brother-in-law among them) captured the Alamo. It is generally accepted that most of the women and children stayed in a room in the southwest corner of the Alamo chapel during the fighting. But in his old age, Ana's son Enrique (who was eight the day the Alamo fell) told a reporter that Ana saw her husband die beside the cannon he was firing and rushed to him.

After the fighting, Ana was interviewed along with the rest of the women. And like them, she was given a blanket and two dollars in silver by Santa Anna. In 1848 she and her children got a land grant in recognition of Gregorio's service at the Alamo.

Ana lived the rest of her life in San Antonio, never remarrying, and died in 1849. Maria never married and died within months of her mother.

Another Alamo survivor, Petra Gonzales, is thought to have been a relative of Ana Esparza. She was an old woman at the time of the Alamo siege. Little else is known about her, but Enrique Esparza always referred to her as "Doña Petra."

Juana Navarro Alsbury and Gertrudis Navarro

Juana and Gertrudis were sisters whose story rivals that of Susanna Dickinson for sheer drama. Juana was born in 1812, and Gertrudis came along about eight years later. After their mother died, the girls went to live with their father's sister, Josefa, who had married Juan Martin de Veramendi, a wealthy Mexican official who eventually became governor of the Mexican state that included San Antonio.

The girls lived in luxury, dividing their time between the Veramendi Palace in San Antonio, a mansion in Saltillo, and a summer home in Monclova. They were well educated, cultured, and enjoyed every luxury that could be had in those days on the Texas frontier. Their cousin Ursula eventually married famed frontiersman James Bowie.

Juana married a fellow named Alejo Perez in the early 1830s, and they had a daughter, Encarnacion, who died in infancy. In the summer of 1833, Juana was pregnant with her second child so she decided not to accompany her husband on a visit to land they owned in Victoria. She also opted out of a trip with her aunt, uncle, and cousin Ursula (who was, by this time, married to Bowie and, by some accounts, mother to his two children) to the family's summer home in Monclova. Instead, she stayed in San Antonio and Gertrudis stayed with her. That decision likely saved the sisters' lives.

By the end of the summer, Juana was a widow thanks to a cholera epidemic that ravaged the territory. The disease also killed her aunt, uncle, and cousin Ursula. (There are conflicting reports about how many children Ursula had with Bowie. But all accounts agree that none lived to adulthood.)

Juana was left alone, pregnant and responsible for the teenaged Gertrudis. Her son, Alejo Jr., was born in early 1834. They lived with Juana's in-laws until January of 1836 when Juana married Dr. Horace Alsbury.

Less than a month after the marriage, Alsbury was dispatched by the Alamo's commander to find reinforcements for the imperiled mission. Before he could return or send for his family, Santa Anna arrived in San Antonio. Juana, Gertrudis, and Alejo were trapped. They fled to the Alamo under the protection of Bowie.

Their family was fractured during the Texas Revolution as some members remained loyal to Mexico and others fought for Texas. Juana and Gertrudis' father, the only son of a prominent family, was a Mexican government official who sided with Mexico during the conflict and fought with Santa Anna. An uncle,

José Antonio Navarro, signed the Texas Declaration of Independence.

While most of the women and children stayed in a room near the southwest corner of the mission's chapel throughout the thirteen-day siege, Juana, Gertrudis, and Alejo hid in a room that opened off the west wall of the mission complex—reportedly at Bowie's insistence.

Many of the Alamo's defenders entrusted their watches and other valuables to Juana for safekeeping, no doubt knowing they would never be able to collect them. It was up to Juana to make sure the men's heirs got the items instead, a mission she failed but through no fault of her own.

While the Alamo fell on March 6, Juana and Gertrudis stayed in their room with Alejo, unarmed but guarded by a Mexican boy and a wounded man named Mitchell. Both defenders intercepted the Mexican soldiers who pushed their way into the room, and both fellows were swiftly bayoneted in front of the horrified women.

The soldiers cursed Juana and Gertrudis then rummaged through their belongings, stealing money, clothing, and jewelry, including all items entrusted to them by the Alamo defenders.

According to Juana's account, an officer ordered the women out of the room and told them to wait in front of a cannon while he fetched a superior officer. Men skirmished around them. Bullets zinged past their heads. Bodies sprawled at their feet.

And unbeknownst to them, Mexican soldiers prepared to fire the cannon behind them.

But before anyone could ignite the big gun's fuse, a second Mexican officer was struck by the incongruity of two women standing with a baby in the midst of the corpses and chaos. He stopped, saw what was happening, and ordered them to safety.

They were taken with the rest of the women and children to the home of a local landowner, and there they were interviewed by Santa Anna. He gave each woman a blanket and two dollars in silver, then he let them go.

There was a major disagreement between Juana and that *other* Alamo survivor, Susanna Dickinson, that was no doubt exacerbated by the racial and social differences between the two women.

Some eyewitnesses, including Susanna, claimed that Juana left the Alamo under a flag of truce two days before the Alamo fell, thanks to the intervention of her father who fought with Santa Anna. But other eyewitness accounts, including those of Juana and Gertrudis, put the women inside the walls of the Alamo until March 6.

After Santa Anna released them, the sisters went to live with their father.

Gertrudis eventually married businessman José Miguel Felipe Cantú on July 26, 1841. They had eight children and lived for a time in San Antonio but later moved to Calaveras. Gertrudis died there in 1895.

Juana was widowed again in the mid-1840s. Some accounts say Alsbury died in a gunfight, while others claim he perished during an escape from a Mexican prison. Juana soon married her first husband's cousin, a man named Juan Perez.

In 1857 she petitioned the state legislature for compensation for her services at the Alamo and for the property she lost there. Her request was granted.

She lived most of the rest of her life in San Antonio but died in July of 1888 at her son's ranch on Salado Creek.

Concepción Losoya and Juana Francisca Melton

Concepción and Juana were yet another mother and daughter who survived the Alamo, but unlike Angelina Dickinson and María de Jesús Castro Esparza, Juana was an adult. Concepción's son (and Juana's brother), José Toribio Losoya, was among the Alamo defenders. Juana's husband, Eliel Melton, was the Alamo's quartermaster.

She was terrified the Mexican troops would punish her for being married to an American. After the battle, as the women waited to be interviewed by the Mexican commander, she asked the other women not to reveal her husband's nationality. Enrique Esparza recalled his mother, Ana, telling Juana not to be afraid.

Victoriana de Salinas and her daughters

Little is known of these women beyond the fact that they survived the Alamo siege. There is some evidence to suggest that at least two of the daughters survived to adulthood and lived in San Antonio.

· Common Law and an Uncommon Woman ·

Harriet Ames Site

Deep in the bayou country of East Texas—so deep it's almost Louisiana, in fact—stands a small monument to a woman who was among the first to assert property rights in Texas based on a common-law marriage.

Harriet is commemorated at **Potter's Point.** The easiest way to get there is to start from Jefferson, a historic little town in East Texas north of Marshall. From Jefferson, take State Highway 49 east to Gray, Texas. If you hit the Louisiana state line, you've gone too far. In Gray—a blip of a town—turn right onto FM 727. There is a brown historical marker sign on SH 49 just before you reach FM 727. Drive about five miles and turn right at the sign for Pine Bluff Estates. This is just before FM 727 makes a wicked curve to the left. There is no street sign, but there is a small white homemade sign pointing toward the historical marker, though it is hard to see from FM 727. The historical marker is about a mile down on the left, next to a green portable building.

This is Potter's Point, part of the land on Caddo Lake that Harriet fought so hard to keep. The marker is a simple granite pillar declaring Harriet "the bravest woman in Texas."

The Life of Harriet Ames

Harriet's story comes mostly from her memoir, and it focuses on her life in Texas. She arrived shortly before the Texas Revolution. Her husband, Solomon C. Page, left her and their two children on an ill-provisioned homestead near Austin Bayou while he went to fight.

Believing her husband had been killed, she went to live with her brother in Brazoria. At some point she met Robert Potter and traveled under his protection on her way to Kentucky where she intended to live with her grandmother. But she never made it past the borders of Texas. Potter was smitten and wanted her to stay with him, but there was a problem—Harriet's husband. He turned up alive, sporting a desire to reconcile.

For a time Harriet refused both men, but Potter eventually convinced her that the marriage to Page was not legal in Texas because it had not been blessed by a priest. She married Potter by a bond agreement—essentially a common-law marriage though such relationships were not legally recognized at the time—and they settled at Potter's Point where they built a house. Potter was, of course, lying (or mistaken, depending on how charitable you're feeling) about the legality of Harriet's first marriage. I vote for "lying." Read on, you'll see why.

Potter was a state legislator and told his new wife he had introduced a law to validate marriages by bond. After he was killed in the Regulator-Moderator War on March 2, 1848, Harriet was surprised to discover that not only was there was no record of any such law, but she had no legal right to her own property.

And adding insult to penury, Potter had left the bulk of his estate to another woman. In a will signed less than a month before his death, he left Sophia Mayfield of Austin much of his land and the house in which Harriet was living with her children—two of whom were Potter's. He left Harriet another piece of land, horses, slaves, the household furnishings, and farming stock. Throughout the papers, he referred to Harriet as Harriet A. Page, not Harriet Potter—an indication that he never considered her his legal wife.

About six months after Potter's death, Harriet married a fellow named Charles Ames. The other woman never sought

Monument to Harriet Potter Ames

title to the land, and Harriet continued living there with Ames for ten years. But then Sophia Mayfield died. Her estate sold the property, and the new owners took Harriet to court to force her off Potter's Point. Harriet won in 1872—thirty years after Robert Potter's death—but the verdict was overturned and sent to the Texas Supreme Court. (By this time Ames had died and Harriet was once again a widow.)

Ultimately it was Potter who lost the case—and the property—for Harriet. Because he never mentioned their children or referred to her as his wife in the will, the judges ruled against her. Harriet had no further recourse.

She went to live with one of her daughters in New Orleans. And there, at the age of eighty-three, she wrote her memoir.

Harriet died in St. Tammany Parish, Louisiana, in 1902.

· Moms Turned Moguls ·

Two of the most successful Texas-born businesses in the last century were started by women. **Mary Kay Ash** planned to retire but had an idea she couldn't ignore. **Nina Baird** had to work to support her family.

Mary Kay Ash Site

The company she started is a respected institution now, but when Mary Kay Ash launched her firm it was revolutionary. Girls *wore* makeup; they didn't start companies to manufacture it.

The best way to get the Mary Kay experience is to visit the **Mary Kay Museum** in the company's corporate headquarters in Addison. It's a 35,000-square-foot room brimming with photos, mementos, awards, and a replica of that first, oh-so-famous pink Cadillac. Tours of the company are available, too.

Hours: 9 A.M. to 5 P.M. Mon.-Fri.
    Guided tours available by appointment 9 A.M. to 4:30 P.M. Tues.-Fri.
Admission: Free
Location: May Kay, Inc. Corporate Headquarters at 16251 N. Dallas Parkway in Addison. From I-35 in downtown Dallas, take the Dallas Tollway north and exit at Keller Springs. The Mary Kay campus is about a half mile on the right.
Phone Number: 972-687-5476
Mailing Address: P.O. Box 799045, Dallas, Texas 75379-9045
Web Address: www.marykay.com

The Life of Mary Kay Ash

Mary Kay did not set out to start a lipstick legacy. She just wanted women to have the same opportunities as men in the business world.

By 1963 she had worked her way onto the board of directors for the World Gift Company—not an insignificant feat in that era—when a man she had trained was promoted over her and given twice her salary. Disgruntled and disgusted, she took early retirement and decided to write a book to help women survive and thrive in the business world.

So sitting at her kitchen table one morning not long after leaving World Gift, she made two lists: one of good business practices she had observed during her career, the other of things that needed improvement. By the time she was done she realized she had just written a blueprint for a successful company. If she couldn't get ahead in a male-dominated company, well then, she decided, she would just start her own firm.

She cleaned out her savings, recruited her twenty-year-old son, and bought the rights to a moisturizer she had discovered and liked. Sense of humor firmly in hand, she launched her new company on September 13, 1963—Friday the 13th. The firm's motto was "God first, family second, and career third."

Mary Kay said she wanted to give women the opportunity to go as far as their abilities and drive would take them. She sent her army of self-directed saleswomen out to conquer the cosmetics field and sold almost $200,000 in products the first year. Her firm now employs more than half a million women worldwide.

Mary Kay Ash has been named to the Texas Business Hall of Fame and the Texas Women's Hall of Fame and is a recipient of the Horatio Alger award.

She became chairman emeritus of her company in 1987.

Mary Kay Ash
Photo courtesy Mary Kay Inc.

Nina Baird Sites

Nina Baird started selling bread to support her family. Almost a century later, her family is still profiting from the company she started.

Mrs Baird's has replicated Mrs. Baird's original kitchen in a small museum space in its corporate headquarters in Fort Worth.

Hours: By appointment
Admission: Free
Location: South Fort Worth, just off Interstate 35 at Sycamore School Road
Phone Number: 817-293-6230
Address: 7301 South Freeway, Fort Worth, TX 76134
Web Address: www.mrsbairds.com/tour.html

Several of Mrs Baird's plants give **factory tours**, and the tours always include little bits of Baird history—not to mention samples of goodies warm from the oven.

Fort Worth Plant

Hours: By appointment only on Mon., Wed., and Fri. (Tour does not include the museum, which is in a different building.)
Admission: Free
Restrictions: Tours must be set up in advance. No children younger than six years old allowed. Tour participants may not wear shorts, sandals, or jewelry. White cotton hairnets furnished by the bakery are worn. No gum or candy. No photography.
Location: South Fort Worth, just off Interstate 35 at Sycamore School Road
Phone Number: 817-615-3050

Address: 7301 South Freeway, Fort Worth, TX 76134
Web Address: www.mrsbairds.com/tour.html

Abilene Plant

Hours: 8:30-11 A.M. on Mon., Wed., Thurs., and Fri.
Admission: Free
Restrictions: Tours must be set up at least two weeks in
   advance. No children younger than six years old
   allowed. Tour participants may not wear shorts, san-
   dals, or jewelry. White cotton hairnets furnished by
   the bakery are worn. No gum or candy. No
   photography.
Location: South Abilene, about one block from the inter-
   section of Treadway Road and S. 27th Street
Phone Number: 915-692-3141, ask for the Tour
   Department
Address: 2701 Palm Street, Abilene, TX 79602
Web Address: www.mrsbairds.com/tour.html

Lubbock Plant

Hours: Midmorning to midafternoon on Thurs. and Fri.
Admission: Free
Restrictions: Tours must be set up at least ten days in
   advance. No children younger than six years old
   allowed. Tour participants may not wear shorts, san-
   dals, or jewelry. White cotton hairnets furnished by
   the bakery are worn. No gum or candy. No
   photography.
Location: Central Lubbock, near the intersection of East
   Broadway and Date Avenue, one block east of Avenue
   A.
Phone Number: 806-763-9304, ask for the Tour
   Department

Address: 202 East Broadway, Lubbock, TX 79408
Web Address: www.mrsbairds.com/tour.html

Waco Plant

Hours: Vary, by appointment
Admission: Free
Restrictions: Tours must be set up in advance. No children
    younger than six years old allowed. Tour participants
    may not wear shorts, sandals, or jewelry.
Location: Central Waco, west of I-35, between Franklin
    Avenue and Mary Avenue on S. 17th Street
Phone Number: 254-753-7381, ask for the Tour
    Department
Address: 225 S. 17th Street, Waco, TX 76701
Web Address: www.mrsbairds.com/tour.html

The Life of Nina Baird

No one ever called her Nina—the woman who became Mrs. Baird to generations of Texans was Ninnie to her family.

She first saw Texas in late 1901 from the windows of a train when her husband, restaurateur William Baird, moved his family from Tennessee to Fort Worth. Within seven years he was so sick with complications from diabetes that he could barely work.

By that time there were eight children in the family, and Ninnie knew she had to find a way to help support them. Her neighbors had always been enthusiastic about the bread and cakes she baked and gave away. Based on that, she reasoned that others might be willing to pay for her baked goods.

With her four sons as delivery boys and her husband as a kitchen helper, Ninnie started selling bread and cakes from her home in 1908. William died in 1911, leaving Ninnie the sole provider for her family.

Ninnie Baird
Photo courtesy of the Baird Family

She baked every day in a wood stove that could handle only four loaves at one time. The fire had to be fed constantly to keep the heat as even as possible. The boys took basketsful of their mother's baked goods and peddled them throughout the neighborhood. Soon, they were "pedaling" in earnest and using their bicycles for deliveries.

Within four years of William's death, Ninnie's business needed to expand so she bought a commercial oven from a hotel. And she drove a hard bargain. Instead of the $75 asking price, she paid $25 in cash and the rest in bread and rolls.

Two more years and the business had expanded beyond bicycles to a buggy and then to a car for deliveries. In one more year the business finally outgrew the Baird home. Ninnie moved it into a building at the intersection of 6th and Terrell in Fort Worth. The new plant expanded nine times in ten years to keep up with demand. Then the business began expanding to other plants.

Over the years Ninnie gave more responsibilities to her sons, but she remained chairman of the board with final say on big decisions. She always kept an office at the original plant, and she was always on hand for the opening of a new facility. Even as her health began to suffer, she insisted on being included in business decisions and convened board meetings at her home.

Ninnie died on June 3, 1961, in Fort Worth. She was ninety-two.

Newspapers across the state carried stories about her life and death, and the Texas Senate passed a resolution declaring that she had been "a living example for mothers, wives, business executives, Christians, and good people the world over."

· The Circus Queen of the Southwest ·

Mollie Bailey Site

Tucked into a little room in a small San Antonio museum is an abbreviated account of the life of Mollie Bailey. The size of the display is in no way representative of the impact she had during her lifetime. Performer, spy, circus owner, and philanthropist—Mollie Bailey always made her presence felt.

No tribute to the circus would be complete without an homage to Mollie—and the **Hertzberg Circus Museum** aims to be complete. On its second floor, in a room devoted to Texans in the circus, Mollie is remembered in an all-too-brief display.

Hours: 10 A.M. to 5 P.M. Mon.-Sat.
1 to 5 P.M. Sunday (June through August)
Admission: $2.50 for adults, $2 for senior citizens, $1 for children 3-12
Location: Downtown San Antonio at the corner of West Market and Presa Streets, three blocks south of the Alamo. From I-35 take the exit towards I-37 and watch for Commerce Street. Exit at Commerce and stay in the left-hand lane. Turn left onto Presa Street, then left again onto West Market Street. The museum is on the right. Free parking is provided across the street.
Phone Number: 210-207-7819
Address: 210 West Market Street, San Antonio, Texas 78205
Web Address: www.sat.lib.tx.us/Hertzberg/hzmain.html

The Life of Mollie Bailey

Mollie was born on a plantation outside Mobile, Alabama, probably on November 2, 1844. The records are sketchy, but that is the generally accepted date. Her family farmed for a living, but that life was not for Miss Mollie. When she was barely thirteen, Mollie eloped with Gus Bailey, a young man who played clarinet in his father's circus band. She literally ran off and joined the circus.

She and Gus sang (and danced) for their supper across the South while performing with The Bailey Family Troupe. Then the Civil War came and Gus joined Hood's Texas Brigade as bandmaster. Rather than be separated from Gus, Mollie joined the brigade as a nurse, leaving her infant daughter with friends in Virigina. She later claimed—and some sources back her up—that she acted as a spy for Gen. John Bell Hood during the war, smuggling quinine packets hidden in her hair through enemy lines.

After the war Mollie and Gus continued to support themselves by performing throughout the South. For a time they traveled by riverboat, but in 1879 they traded the boat in Texas for a one-ring circus. They dubbed it "The Bailey Circus, A Texas Show for Texas People." But when Gus became ill and stopped traveling with the circus, it was rechristened the Mollie A. Bailey Show.

Mollie endeared herself to Texas communities by giving free tickets to war veterans (from any side of any war) and poor children. She bought land throughout the state so the circus could perform on its own land, thereby avoiding the exorbitant occupation taxes often levied by towns on traveling shows that set up in public places. Mollie allowed civic and church groups to use the properties free of charge when the circus was not in town—something else that endeared her to Texans for decades.

Mollie Bailey
Photo courtesy of the Hertzberg Circus Museum

At its grandest, Mollie's show had at least thirty-one wagons and more than two hundred animals including elephants and camels. Mollie was an entertainer who enjoyed the spotlight and her role as circus doyenne. She insisted on looking the part and always wore a hat that was more costume than fashion.

She and Gus had nine children together, and the kids split their time between the circus' winter quarters in Blum, where Gus lived, and traveling with Mollie. Gus died in 1896.

Mollie remarried ten years later to a man who ran the show's gaslights. He was much younger than Mollie and took her name when they wed—Blackie Hardesty became Blackie Bailey.

Mollie retired from the road in 1917 and died the following year in Houston.

· Capital Women ·

Austin, the Texas state capital, is an important place for women. It is, after all, the place where state laws were passed that gave women the right to vote, own property, and be treated as equals to men under state law.

It is also where the state's first woman governor, **Miriam "Ma" Ferguson**, served her two terms in office and where the redoubtable **Minnie Fisher Cunningham** led the fight for womans suffrage in Texas. It's where **Barbara Jordan**, the first black woman elected to statewide office, served before moving on to national office and national prominence with the Watergate hearings, and it is where **Annie Webb Blanton**, the first woman ever elected to statewide office, served too.

The Texas State Capitol

You will not find a display in the **state capitol** building about the amazing women who have walked its halls, but it is worth a visit to the building just to saunter a bit in their footsteps. Talk with the guards, clerks, tour guides, and others who work there. Many are happy to tell stories—some real, some embellished—about the likes of Ma Ferguson and Barbara Jordan.

The building is also the site of a famous statue of Stephen F. Austin by renowned sculptor **Elizabet Ney**. (More about her later in The Artist's Way chapter.) Another interesting note— an extensive renovation of the capitol in the early 1990s was headed by **Dealey Herndon,** the same woman who later managed construction of The Women's Museum: An Institute for the Future, in Dallas.

Guided tours of the capitol are available.

The Texas State Capitol
Photo courtesy of the Austin Convention and Visitors Bureau

Public Visiting Hours: 7 A.M. to 10 P.M. Mon.-Fri., 9 A.M.
    to 5 P.M. Sat.-Sun.
Guided Tour Hours: 8:30 A.M. to 4:30 P.M. Mon.-Fri., 9:30
    A.M. to 4:30 P.M. Sat.-Sun.
Admission: Free
Location: It's hard to miss from just about anyplace in
    downtown Austin. Guided tours begin outside the
    Capitol Information Center, which is in the south
    foyer just inside the building's main entrance. Tours
    begin every fifteen minutes and last about forty-five
    minutes. Reservations are only required for groups of
    ten or more.
Phone Number: Capitol Information and Guide Service,
    512-463-0063

Address: 13ᵗʰ and Congress Avenue
Web Address: www.thc.state.tx.us/travel/statecapitol.html

Miriam Ferguson Sites

Long before she became known as "Ma" or as Madame Governor, Miriam Ferguson was a belle of Belton, Texas. The **Bell County Museum** in her home county offers photos and information about her in two displays on its first floor.

> *Hours*: 1 to 5 P.M. Tues.-Sat. Group tours and other hours by appointment.
> *Admission*: Free
> *Location*: 201 North Main Street in downtown Belton, about two blocks from the courthouse square. Take I-35 to Belton, just south of Temple, and take exit 294A. Turn right (if you're driving from the north, left if from the south) onto E. Central Avenue. Drive past the courthouse square. Turn right onto Main Street. The museum is one-tenth of a mile on the right. Parking is in the back.
> *Phone Number*: 254-933-5243
> *Mailing Address*: P.O. Box 1381, Belton, Texas 76513
> *Web Address*: www.vvm.com/~museum/

She is buried next to her husband, who was also a Texas governor, in the **Texas State Cemetery**, 909 Navasota Street, in Austin. 512-463-0605. An imposing gravestone—suitable for a two-governor family—marks the site.

The Life of Miriam "Ma" Ferguson

Miriam Ferguson was an unexpected trailblazer who left a complicated legacy. She was the first woman governor of Texas and only the second woman to win a gubernatorial race nationwide. She fought the Ku Klux Klan, was accused of taking kickbacks, and championed a state sales tax during her terms in office. It was not the life she was raised to pursue.

Women couldn't even vote when Miriam Amanda Wallace was born in Bell County, Texas, on June 13, 1875. She had no early aspirations for a career in politics—or any career at all outside the home. Upper middle class girls like Miriam were expected to be accomplished, marry well, have children, and make a home. And for a while, it seemed that was the path Miriam was taking. She attended Salado College (a preparatory school) and Baylor Female College before marrying lawyer and fellow Bell County native James Edward Ferguson in 1899. They had two daughters. She made a home for them.

She became the First Lady of Texas when her husband was elected governor in 1915. He was impeached two years later and banned from holding state office again. That did not stop him from running for other posts, but he always lost.

Finally he induced his wife to run for governor in 1924 as a Democrat. He ran her campaign. Ironically, while governor he had been an ardent opponent of woman's suffrage.

It was during her first run for governor that Miriam became "Ma" Ferguson. Some point to the obvious and say she was the "Ma" to her husband's "Pa," but others claim the moniker came from combining the initials of her first and middle names. Regardless, the name stuck and today many Texans can tell you that "Ma" Ferguson was governor, but few will recognize the name Miriam Ferguson. She ran on a platform promising "two governors for the price of one" and was elected easily in November of 1924. She narrowly missed being the first woman governor ever in the United States: Nellie Ross was sworn in

Miriam A. Ferguson delivering her speech at her inauguration.
House of Representatives Chamber, Capitol Building,
Austin, Texas. January 20, 1925.
Photo courtesy The UT Institute of Texan Cultures at San Antonio,
The San Antonio Light Collection.

as governor of Wyoming a mere fifteen days before Ma took the oath in Texas.

Despite the fact that she ran essentially to get her husband into the governor's mansion through the back door, Ma did take an active interest and prominent role in her first administration—an administration riddled by controversy. During her campaign she had promised to fight the KKK, and she followed through by championing an anti-mask measure in the legislature. But such accomplishments were overshadowed by accusations that the Fergusons took kickbacks on state highway contracts and granted questionable prison pardons and paroles. Ma was threatened with impeachment, but that never happened. However, she did lose her bid for re-election. In fact, she did not even get her party's nomination for the office that year.

She lost a third bid for governor in 1930. But in 1932, as the Great Depression gripped Texas, her promises of tax cuts found receptive listeners and she was elected to a second term. It was a much quieter tenure in office, with no major controversies even though she continued her generous dispersal of paroles and pardons. Ma opted not to seek re-election after her second term. But in 1940 she ran one last time and lost.

She was widowed four years later and never ran for public office again. Instead, she lived quietly in Austin until 1961, when she died of heart failure on June 25 at the age of eighty-six.

Minnie Fisher Cunningham Sites

One of the homes where Minnie Fisher lived in Galveston is still standing. The white-columned bungalow at 3128 Avenue O½, just a few blocks from the seawall, is in private hands so there are no public tours. It is easy to find, as that part of Galveston was laid out in a simple grid pattern. For the alphabetically challenged, Avenue O½ is between Avenue O and Avenue P.

Minnie Fisher moved to Galveston to attend pharmacy school and was the third woman to graduate from the University of Texas Medical Branch's pharmacy program. She attended classes in the **Ashbel Smith Building**, commonly called "Old Red" because of the color of the stone used to construct it. The building is at 902-928 Strand—basically it's where Strand dead

Minnie Fisher Cunningham once lived in this Galveston house.

ends into the UTMB campus. The building earned its nickname honestly and it's hard to miss. The school graduated many of the state's first women doctors, dentists, and pharmacists.

The Life of Minnie Fisher Cunningham

Minnie Fisher Cunningham is best known for leading the fight for woman suffrage in Texas, but those activities are just a fraction of what she did in her lifetime. In a state chockfull of colorful and controversial characters, Minnie Fish—as she was known to her pals—more than holds her own in the history books.

Born on March 19, 1882, to Horatio and Sallie Fisher on the family farm near New Waverly, she came by her zeal for public service naturally—her father was active in local politics and served in the Texas House of Representatives from 1857 to 1858.

For her own career, Minnie first chose teaching, but that lasted only a year before she enrolled in the pharmacy school at the University of Texas Medical Branch at Galveston. In 1901 she became the third woman to receive a pharmacy degree in the state of Texas. She went to work in a pharmacy in Huntsville, but was incensed when she found out she was being paid half the amount her male colleagues were earning. That experience convinced her to join a local suffrage organization— the beginning of her fight for women's equality.

She married lawyer Bill Cunningham in 1902. When she moved with him to Galveston in 1907, she continued her work on behalf of suffrage and in 1910 was elected president of the Galveston Equal Suffrage Association. In 1915 she was elected president of the Texas Woman Suffrage Association, and two years later she moved to Austin in order to fight for her cause near the seat of state government.

It was under her leadership that the state suffrage movement really took off. The suffragettes organized letter-writing campaigns and lobbying groups. Membership ballooned.

In 1919, when the battle was on to pass the Nineteenth Amendment to the U.S. Constitution (which gave women the right to vote), Minnie Fish traveled the country stirring up support for the measure. When the time came for her home state to ratify it, she returned to Austin and monitored the train station the night of the vote so opponents of the amendment could not prevent a quorum by spiriting lawmakers away. On June 28, 1919, Texas became the ninth state—and first in the South—to adopt the 19th Amendment.

The same year women got the vote, Minnie Fish helped organize the National League of Women Voters. She remained an active member for most of the rest of her life.

For much of the 1920s, she split her time between Washington, D.C. and Texas. By that time she and her husband spent most of their time apart. She was a workaholic; he was an alcoholic; they had no children. Minnie saw no reason to live together under those circumstances, but she always spoke well of her husband in public and gave him credit for supporting her—emotionally and financially—in all her endeavors. She returned to Texas when her husband died in 1927.

The following year she made her first unsuccessful run for office. She was the first woman to run for a seat in the United States Senate from Texas, but she made a dismal showing in the primary—placing fifth in the slate of six candidates.

She was a fierce Democrat and loyal supporter of President Franklin D. Roosevelt. Some say it was FDR who dubbed her "Minnie Fish." In 1939 she moved back to Washington, D.C. to work for the Agricultural Adjustment Administration, but she resigned in 1943 to protest a rule she felt kept farmers from getting information they needed.

The following year, in a fury over the incumbent governor's lack of support for FDR, Minnie Fish ran for governor. She lost the Democratic primary to the incumbent but made a better showing this time—second in a slate of nine.

It was the last time she sought public office, but not the end of her involvement in politics. She remained an energetic operator for the Democratic Party and liberal causes. She started Democrats of Texas, campaigned for Adlai Stevenson and John F. Kennedy for president, unsuccessfully challenged Texas Senator Lyndon Johnson for the chairmanship of the state delegation to the Democratic National Convention, supported civil rights candidates and legislation, and helped start the *Texas Observer*.

Often for Minnie, "fighting the good fight" was enough—sometimes it was even the point. In the midst of her battle with LBJ over leadership of the state delegation to the Democratic convention, a reporter asked her if she thought she could win. Minnie's answer? "What do you call winning?" It wasn't the first time she started a battle to draw attention to an issue.

Minnie Fish died in New Waverly on December 9, 1964, at the age of eighty-two.

1944 Campaign Poster for Minnie Fisher Cunningham's last run for public office.

Barbara Jordan Sites

Like Ma Ferguson, Barbara Jordan is buried in the **Texas State Cemetery**, 909 Navasota Street, in Austin. 512-463-0605. The word "PATRIOT" is emblazoned across the top of her headstone.

Her archives are at her alma mater, Texas Southern University, in Houston.

Hours: 8 A.M. to 5 P.M. Mon.-Fri.
Admission: Free
Location: The Robert James Terry Library on the TSU campus
Phone Number: 713-313-7011
Address: 3100 Cleburne Avenue, Houston, TX 77004
Web Address: www.tsu.edu/library/special.htm

The Life of Barbara Jordan

The story of Barbara Jordan's life is a good old-fashioned American success story. Born in the midst of the Great Depression in Houston's Fourth Ward, she overcame prejudice, economic disadvantage, and illness to become a U.S. Representative to Congress, the first black woman elected to the state senate, a star of the Democratic Party, and an inspiration to generations.

The youngest of three daughters of a Houston homemaker and a Baptist minister, Barbara Charline Jordan was born on February 21, 1936. Her parents valued education and encouraged their children to better their lives through learning. Barbara was a stellar pupil in the public schools and went on to attend Texas Southern University.

After graduating from TSU with highest honors in 1956, she went to law school at Boston University and received her degree in 1959. She returned to Houston to start her law

Barbara Jordan in 1966
Photo courtesy of The UT Institute of Texan Cultures at San Antonio.

practice the following year. Her parents, ever helpful, let her live with them and operate her law practice out of their home until she could save enough money for an office. It took three years.

During that time she got involved in local politics and organized drives to get African Americans registered to vote. Aided by a big voice that she used with precision for causes she believed in, Barbara began to garner the attention of the public and local politicians. She ran unsuccessfully for the state senate twice before finally landing the job in 1967. She was the first black state senator in Texas since 1883, and the first black woman senator in state history. Imagine it—at the height of the Civil Rights Movement there was Barbara along with thirty white men trying to make a difference for her constituents. What are the chances she would be successful?

But she was. She continued her voter registration efforts and worked hard for minimum wage laws. Thorough as ever, Barbara never attended a committee meeting or a senate session unprepared. Not only did she earn her colleagues' respect, she earned their loyalty. In 1972 they elected her president pro tempore of the Texas Senate. The vote was unanimous.

The following year, with the backing of Lyndon Baines Johnson and the state Democratic Party, Barbara sought and captured a seat in the United States House of Representatives. She was the first African American woman from a Southern state ever elected to the House.

Hers became a household name in 1974 when she served on the House Judiciary Committee during the Watergate hearings. She was tapped to give the keynote address at the Democratic National Convention two years later, and again in 1992.

By then she was long retired from Congress. She left in 1979 to take a teaching job at the University of Texas in the LBJ School of Public Affairs. Though active in politics behind the scenes, she never again ran for public office.

Multiple sclerosis confined her to a wheelchair toward the end of her life. She died in Austin of complications from leukemia on January 17, 1996.

Annie Blanton Site

Annie is buried in **Oakwood Cemetery** in Austin, 1601 Navasota Street. The cemetery is directly across Interstate 35 from the University of Texas main campus.

The Life of Annie Webb Blanton

Houston native Annie Webb Blanton is the least known of these Capital Women, but her contribution cannot be—should not be—underrated. She was the first woman ever elected to a statewide office in Texas.

Women had just gained the right to vote in primaries in 1918 when Annie ran for state superintendent of public instruction. She was certainly qualified for the job—a respected teacher who had become the first woman president of the Texas State Teachers Association and was vice president of the National Education Association. But the fact that she was a woman disqualified her in the eyes of many. And her activities as a suffragist had earned her many enemies.

It was a bitter, nasty campaign. Among other things, her opponents accused her of being an atheist. (She was, in fact, a lifelong Methodist.) Despite the smear tactics, and with the help of all those newly minted women voters, Annie won.

Annie was one of Thomas and Eugenia Webb Blanton's seven children. She and her twin, Fannie, were born August 19, 1870. After graduating from La Grange High School in 1886, she worked as a teacher while putting herself through the University of Texas. It took almost thirteen years while working full time, but she finally graduated in 1899.

Afterward, she started teaching English at the college level (at North Texas State Normal College—now the University of North Texas). Between 1900 and 1918—the year she was elected state superintendent of public instruction—Annie taught, wrote grammar textbooks, became active in the suffrage movement, and joined the Texas State Teachers Association.

While she was state superintendent of public instruction, Annie worked to improve teacher qualifications and pay, get more money for the schools, and provide free textbooks in public schools. She easily won a second term but opted not to run for a third. Instead, she vied unsuccessfully for a seat in Congress from Denton County.

After losing that race, Annie went back to the University of Texas to get a master's degree and then taught at UT until 1926 when she left to pursue a Ph.D. She returned to UT, degree in hand, in 1927 and taught there for the rest of her career. In 1929 she founded an honorary society for women teachers called Delta Kappa Gamma Society.

Annie Webb Blanton died October 2, 1945, in Austin.

· From Half Time to the Big Time ·

Gussie Nell Davis and Rangerettes Site

In the year before the United States joined World War II, a P.E. teacher from a small Texas town accepted a challenge from a small Texas college and started a phenomenon that is still going strong today: the drill team. There had been nothing like it before, but there have been thousands like it since. Many people helped make the Kilgore College Rangerettes a sensation, but all help flowed through Gussie Nell Davis.

Kilgore College maintains a **Rangerette Showcase and Museum** that includes costumes, photographs, clippings, videos, a mechanized display of props, and a tribute to Gussie Nell Davis.

Hours: 9 A.M. to 4 P.M. Mon.-Fri., 10 A.M. to 4 P.M. Sat., Closed Sundays

Admission: Free—group tours by appointment only

Location: Physical Education Complex (at the intersection of Broadway and Ross on the Kilgore College campus, one block west of State Highway 259)

Phone Number: 903-983-8265

Address: 1100 Broadway, Kilgore, TX 75662-3299

Web Address: www.kilgore.cc.tx.us/attr/ranshow/ ranshow.html

The Life of Gussie Nell Davis and the Kilgore College Rangerettes

It was a simple concept: give folks something to watch during half time at Kilgore College football games. But Dean B.E. Masters didn't want just any ol' pep squad or drum corps. This was the 1940s and he wanted something different, something "so good that it will keep people in the stands, that they won't want to leave."

Enter Gussie Nell Davis, a maverick teacher who had combined music, dance, and rigorous physical training to form the Flaming Flashes, a pep squad at Greenville High School whose members used flaming batons and flags in addition to the more traditional drums and bugles. She took up Masters' challenge.

On September 19, 1940, under a sky blazing with fireworks, forty-eight Rangerettes marched onto the field and launched a worldwide trend. Clad in red, white, and blue, with their skirts a daring two inches above the knee, the girls "pirouetted, pranced, danced in perfect unison, colorful in movement and attire..." reported the *Kilgore Daily News*.

According to *A History of Kilgore College*, "Miss Davis remembers the deafening silence that followed the presentation. Her heart was in her throat, and she wondered if she would ever get another job. Then the cheering and applause began."

The modern drill team had been born.

Since then, the Rangerettes have performed around the world—at fairs, presidential inaugurations, parades, festivals, and of course, football games. In 2000 the group performed at its fiftieth consecutive Cotton Bowl. (In 1999 Gussie Nell Davis became the first woman inducted into the Cotton Bowl Hall of Fame.)

Sportscaster Red Grange dubbed them the "Sweethearts of the Gridiron" in 1950, and their performances were judged as

The Rangerettes with Lyndon Johnson in Washington, D.C.
Photo courtesy of Kilgore College

better than those of the Rockettes. The Rangerettes soon developed a few signature moves—the jump splits and a high kick in which each girl's leg touches the brim of her white Western hat. Those hats, along with white belts and boots, red shirts, and "flippy" blue skirts, are part of a uniform that has actually been copyrighted.

Gussie Nell, the little girl from Farmersville, took a job and turned it into a lifelong passion. Born November 4, 1906, to Robert and Mattie Davis, she had attended public schools in Farmersville and nurtured a desire to be a concert pianist. That was still the plan when she began classes at the College of Industrial Arts (now Texas Woman's University) in 1923, but she soon changed her major to physical education. The year after getting her bachelor's degree in 1927, she took the job at Greenville High School that garnered the attention of Kilgore College. She eventually got a master's degree from the University of Southern California in 1938.

Gussie Nell Davis
Photo courtesy of Kilgore College

Gussie Nell stayed with Kilgore College and the Rangerettes until her retirement in 1979. She also founded American Drill Team Schools, Inc., with Irving Dreibrodt, former director of the SMU Mustang Band. She worked as a drill team consultant and judged drill team competitions and was a member of the National Drill Team Directors Association.

In all that time she received scores of accolades. She also got heaps of criticism from those who saw the Rangerettes as nothing more than "sexist...mindless...Barbie Dolls," a view she turned aside by opining that there was nothing wrong in learning self-confidence, discipline, cooperation, and the ability to perform precision dance, along with poise, etiquette, and personal grooming. She was also criticized for her failure to include African Americans in the group. The first black Rangerette joined the group in 1973.

Gussie Nell died on December 20, 1993, in Kilgore. She was buried in Farmersville Cemetery.

· Panhandle Mystery Woman ·

Frenchy McCormick Sites

Frenchy McCormick is a true Texas legend, a woman with a mysterious past who lived alone in a ghost town for a quarter century rather than leave her husband's grave. She lived on land that now belongs to Cal Farley's Boys Ranch.

The Old Courthouse Museum at Cal Farley's Boys Ranch devotes a second-floor corner to Frenchy and her legendary life.

> *Hours*: 8 A.M. to 5 P.M. daily. If the museum is locked, walk across the street to the ranch's administration building and ask for the key.
>
> *Admission*: Free
>
> *Location*: Cal Farley's Boys Ranch. To get there from Amarillo, take the Bell Street exit off Interstate 40 and go north. Turn left on FM 1061 (there's a Sonic at the intersection). Proceed about 35 miles to where it dead ends into Highway 385. Turn right. The ranch is about three miles on the right. Turn into the entrance and proceed through the gates. The administration building is on the right, the museum on the left.
>
> *Phone Number*: 806-534-2200
>
> *Address*: P.O. Box 1890, Amarillo, TX 79174
>
> *Web Address*: None

Just outside the gates of the ranch, on the right if you're leaving the property, is a twisted old cottonwood tree. Frenchy's adobe house used to stand under it. The ranch hopes to someday re-create it.

Frenchy is buried next to her husband in the **Casimero Romero Cemetery**. It's on a neighboring property to the ranch, but ranch staff have permission to go there and are happy to take visitors. It's best to call ahead for an appointment: Darci Johnson at 806-373-6600 ext. 635 or Mike Pacino at 806-534-2200 ext. 202.

The Life of Frenchy McCormick

Frenchy McCormick was probably born about 1852 somewhere in Louisiana. No one knows for sure, as she always refused to talk about her past. In one popular tale about her early life, she ran away from a convent school in Baton Rouge with a man who later abandoned her.

According to another tale, her mother died in Baton Rouge when she was very young. Frenchy was left in the care of her father, who owned a steamboat that operated on the Mississippi River. She allegedly quarreled with him because she wanted to dance on the stage—a scandalous career for a well-bred young lady at that time. When he refused to allow it, Frenchy caught a stage to Dodge City where she danced in saloons.

She spoke French fluently, and as the story goes, a cowboy in one of those establishments exclaimed, "I want to dance with Frenchy!" Thereafter, she was known by everyone as Frenchy—everyone except her husband. He always called her Elizabeth.

Frenchy met her future husband, Mickey McCormick, at the gaming tables in Mobeetie—a town near Fort Elliott in the Texas Panhandle—around 1880. The Irish-born gambler claimed he always won when she was near because she brought him luck. McCormick lived in the wild frontier town of Tascosa, and when he went back there Frenchy went with him. She always called him Mack.

They were married in 1881. The name Frenchy gave for the marriage certificate was Elizabeth McGraw.

FRENCHY McCORMICK, THE LAST
RESIDENT OF OLD TASCOSA,
PHOTOGRAPHED ABOUT 1940.

Elizabeth "Frenchy" McCormick, circa 1940
Photo courtesy of Cal Farley's Boys Ranch

She worked in a local saloon and dealt monte in a gambling room behind it. Mickey built them a two-room adobe house under a cottonwood tree a few blocks from a livery stable he owned. Their mutual affection was well known and oft remarked on in the town. When Mickey was out of town, he frequently sent letters home. When one arrived, Frenchy would tell neighbors, "I heard from Mack!"

For a time they prospered, however the town declined steadily after the railroad bypassed it in 1887. But the McCormicks had pledged to stay together and stay in Tascosa, so that is what they did. Frenchy was widowed on October 7, 1912, and buried her husband in a cemetery on a nearby hill. She could see his gravestone from her front yard.

In 1915 the county seat moved from Tascosa to Vega, and with it went most of the town's residents—everyone but Frenchy. She refused to leave her home. She refused to leave "my Mack." For twenty-seven years she lived in her slowly deteriorating house with no running water, no electricity, and no near neighbors. People would check on her from time to time to make sure she was safe and had food.

By the end of her life, she had become a legend. It was obvious to people that she was educated: She was well spoken and had lovely handwriting. But she still refused to reveal anything about her past. That only added to the legend. Here was a once beautiful, educated woman who chose to live in poverty in a ghost town near her dead husband's grave rather than leave.

People began to visit her from all over the United States, some with less than honorable motives. Friends of Frenchy's once arrived to find two men from an eastern university ransacking her trunks while a dazed Frenchy clutched her torn marriage certificate.

She was finally convinced to leave Tascosa in 1939 to live with friends in nearby Channing. She died there after a bout with pneumonia on January 12, 1941. She was buried at noon the next day beside her Mack.

The graves of Frenchy and Mickey McCormick (foreground) near Cal Farley's Boys Ranch. Frenchy's is the shorter of the two.

Frenchy reportedly once said, "No one will ever find out who I am." No one ever did.

· Bird Lady of Texas ·

Connie Hagar Sites

Connie Hagar is a good example of what can happen when someone has a cause and pursues it passionately. Connie's passion was birds, and as a result Texas has a wildlife sanctuary and a body of knowledge it wouldn't have had without her. Her zeal for chronicling the Texas coastal bird migrations in the 1930s brought worldwide attention to the birds and to Connie.

The **Connie Hagar Wildlife Sanctuary,** maintained by the Texas Department of Parks and Wildlife (there's really not much to maintain), encompasses a marshy roadside area along Business 35 in Rockport. The sanctuary extends into the waters of Little Bay. This was one of Connie's favorite daily birding stops. A variety of birds can be seen there throughout the year. Outdoors along Texas 35 (note: NOT Interstate 35, this is a state road), it is on the left, just as you enter Rockport from the north. You literally have to go through a McDonald's parking lot to get to it. There is a **historical marker** nearby dedicated to Connie. Usually a person must be dead at least twenty years before qualifying for a state historical marker, but the State Historical Commission waived that rule for Connie, and the marker was dedicated on September 8, 1990, seventeen years after her death.

The Connie Hagar Wildlife Sanctuary at Little Bay in Rockport

Connie is buried next to her husband in **Rockport Cemetery**, in a spot that overlooks the Connie Hagar Wildlife Sanctuary.

The **Connie Hagar Cottage Sanctuary** in Rockport is on the former site of a small motel complex once owned by Connie and her husband, Jack. Connie watched the birds while Jack took care of the guests. Ornithologists from around the world traveled to Rockport and stayed with the Hagars while studying the coastal Texas bird migrations. After Connie's death, the Friends of Connie Hagar bought the property, established the sanctuary, and maintain it. The cottages are gone (though you can see where they were), but the six-acre site still attracts an impressive number of feathered visitors—grosbeaks, warblers, flycatchers, thrushes, vireos, sparrows, and buntings. Folks who know about such things say it's a great place for birding. It was one of the first sites established on The Great Texas Coastal Birding Trail, which eventually will link more than fifty sites in communities from Brownsville to Beaumont.

Even if birding isn't your bag, the sanctuary is a great place to take a walk on the wild side. Trails loop throughout the property's fields and woods.

An observation platform and bird feeder at the
Connnie Hagar Cottage Sanctuary in Rockport

Hours: Sunrise to sunset

Admission: Free

Location: On the south side of Rockport. Heading south on Texas Highway 35, you can drive through town or take the bypass around the main part of Rockport. Take a left at Market Street and a right onto Church Street. The sanctuary is in a residential area at the intersection of Church and First Street.

Phone Number: None

Address: None

Web Address: www.ohwy.com/tx/c/cohacosa.htm

The Life of Connie Hagar

Conger "Connie" Neblett was born in Corsicana, Texas, on June 14, 1886, to Robert and Mattie Neblett. After graduating from Corsicana High School in 1903, she studied music at Forest Park College in Saint Louis, the University of Chicago, and the American Conservatory. She was a talented singer and pianist but thought a career in music unseemly for a well-bred young woman, so she turned down an offer to sing for her supper.

A brief, unhappy first marriage ended in 1921. Five years later she married Bostonian Jack Hagar. The couple moved to Rockport in 1935.

Connie got her first real experience with birds shortly after World War I when she volunteered to band birds for the United States Biological Survey. The birds around her new home in coastal Texas fascinated her, and Connie began studying them in earnest.

Through the years she identified twenty new species of birds native to Texas and was the first to report on the visits of many migratory species on the Texas coast, including a few thought to be extinct. She was the first birder to chronicle the great migrations of birds along the Texas coast, and her observations were published in a number of ornithology journals.

She was an amateur ornithologist, but she gained the respect of the top U.S. and European scientists in the field. An ardent conservationist, she frequently talked about her studies and the need for protecting the birds: Her audiences included everyone from school children and civic club members to scientists.

Life magazine did a story about her in 1956, and the pictures show her in her normal birding attire—starched linen. The photographer complained that she didn't look like a bird watcher, though there is no record of how exactly he expected a bird watcher to appear.

In 1962 the National Audubon Society convened its annual meeting in Corpus Christi, reportedly so Connie (who was seventy-six years old by that time) could attend. She received a special citation from the society that year. That same year she was widowed when Jack died of a stroke at the age of eighty-five. Not long afterward her own health began to fail, and she slid into a long illness. Connie spent the last two years of her life blind, and she died in a Corpus Christi nursing home on November 29, 1973, at the age of eighty-six.

· Pioneer and Town Founder ·

Margaret Hallett Sites

Hallettsville sits tucked away between Houston and San Antonio in a part of Texas that was part of Stephen F. Austin's original colony: It has the distinction of being one of the few towns in Texas named in honor of a woman. She donated the land for the town, lived there, and is buried there. *Ripley's Believe It Or Not!* dubbed Hallettsville "13 City" because in 1913 it had 13 letters in its name, 1,300 residents, 13 churches, 13 newspapers, and 13 saloons.

Hallettsville Garden and Cultural Center is on the site of the original estate granted by Stephen F. Austin to Margaret's husband, John. The cabin John built here was the first settler's home in the area, but he died shortly after it was completed and likely never lived in it. Margaret moved into the cabin with their daughter in 1836. She converted her new home into a trading post, farmed the land around it, and raised horses under her own brand. This is a lovely park, complete with trails and picnic tables, at the corner of West La Grange and Crockett Streets. To get there, take ALT 90 into town and turn north onto La Grange Street. Follow it for about eight blocks (a few of them are long blocks) to where it intersects with Crockett Street.

The Lavaca Historical Museum is devoted to the history of Lavaca County and Hallettsville. It has some information about the founding of the town.

Hours: 1 to 5 P.M. Mon.-Tues. and Thurs.-Fri.
By appointment only on weekends
Closed Wednesdays.
Admission: Free
Location: From ALT 90, turn north onto Main Street. The museum is on the left between First Street and Rogers Street.
Phone Number: 361-798-4113
Address: 413 N. Main Street, Hallettsville, TX 77964
Web Address: None

Margaret Hallett is buried in **Memorial Park Cemetery**. There is a historical marker in the cemetery. A plaque on her grave marker states that she is the widow of a veteran of the Battle of San Jacinto, but that is incorrect. Her son, John Jr., fought in that battle.

Hours: Sunrise to sunset
Admission: Free
Location: From ALT 90, turn south onto South Dowling Street. The cemetery is two-and-a-half blocks down on the right.
Phone Number: None
Address: 313 S. Dowling Street, Hallettsville, TX 77964
Web Address: None

The Life of Margaret Hallett

Margaret Leatherbury Hallett was born Christmas Day of 1787 into a well-to-do Virginia family. When she was eighteen years old, she defied her parents and ran off with John Hallett, an English-born seaman who had been adopted by an American sea captain. During the first few years of their marriage, they lived in New York and Baltimore, and John fought against the British in the War of 1812. He became a sea captain in his own right, but after losing a ship in the Florida Keys he quit the sea,

Margaret Hallett is buried in Memorial Park Cemetery in Hallettsville.

and the Halletts moved to Mexico where they used the insurance money from the lost ship to open a store. After it was confiscated by the Mexican government, the Halletts moved to Goliad in Texas (which was, at that time, still part of Mexico). There, they opened another store and resumed their lives as merchants and traders. John also served as Goliad town clerk.

They had four children together: John Jr., born in 1812; William Henry, born in 1815; Benjamin, born in 1818; and Mary Jane, born in 1822. Benjamin had died by 1824. According to one popular story he was abducted by Indians, but there is no proof of that tale.

In 1833 Stephen F. Austin granted John Hallett a league of land in his colony on the east bank of the Lavaca River. The Halletts hired men to build a cabin for them there, but John died in 1836, before the family could move into it.

Margaret and fourteen-year-old Mary Jane fled the area in 1836 along with other Texas residents as Texas fought for independence from Mexico. It was a tough year for the Halletts. Margaret's son William Henry died, allegedly in Mexico where he had been imprisoned as a spy. When Margaret and her daughter returned to their homestead later that year, they found the place looted and had to contend with squatters.

The following year, Margaret's oldest son, John Jr., was killed in a skirmish with Native Americans.

Margaret was a fifty-year-old widow with a teenage daughter in a hostile environment at a time when women had few rights and fewer opportunities.

Drawing on her past, the feisty widow turned the cabin into a trading post. She traded with the white settlers and learned enough of the Tonkawa Indian language to trade with them, too. One oft-told story has her whacking a larcenous Tonkawan brave in the head with a hatchet. The Tonkawa chief is said to have praised her actions, dubbed her "Brave Squaw," and made her an honorary member of his tribe.

During this time Margaret planted the acreage around her store and grew food for her own use and for trade. She also began raising horses and cattle under her own brand.

By 1838 Texas had won its independence and a settlement was growing around Margaret's store. She donated land for a town, which was named Hallettsville in her honor. She was proud of the town and became a vigorous civic booster. She built a new home in the town and hosted court sessions there until a county seat was established. She also donated land for the town's first public school and a cemetery.

Despite the rugged conditions, Margaret always dressed well and carried a handbag. She was described by one neighbor as "a most intelligent lady, a great reader and well posted, though in a measure self-educated." Legend has it that a newcomer once asked what she carried in the handbag and Margaret replied, "powder, but not of the cosmetic variety."

By the time she died in 1863 at the age of seventy-five, Margaret was a legend in the area and often referred to as "Mother Hallett." She was buried near her home, but her remains were later moved to Memorial Park.

· Teacher, Rancher, and Chili Cook-off Queen ·

Hallie Stillwell Site

Some people keep scrapbooks. Hallie started a museum to preserve her memories. And what memories they were! From shooting cougars to riding herd on cattle and dodging desperadoes, writing a newspaper column to presiding over an annual chili cook-off. She didn't do it all but she did a lot—enough to make her a Texas legend.

Hallie's Hall of Fame Museum honors Hallie's memory and preserves memorabilia from her long, interesting life. Opened in 1991, on her ninety-fourth birthday, the museum (built with adobe bricks made on the ranch) is filled with photos, her many awards, and artifacts such as her barber license and candle-making equipment. There is also a replica of the one-room cabin she went to as a bride.

> *Hours*: Always available to visitors. Just go to the store next door and ask for the key. The person who gives it to you might be one of Hallie's descendants.
> *Admission*: Free
> *Location*: This is as close to the middle of nowhere as you're likely to get. It's 29 miles north of Big Bend National Park. From Big Bend, or from the town of Marathon, take Highway 385 to FM 2627. Go east (it's the only way you can turn) and proceed about six miles. It's a narrow, hilly road so drive slowly. Hallie's Hall of Fame is on the right next to a store and RV park on the grounds of the Stillwell Ranch.

Phone Number: 915-576-2244
Address: HC-65, Box 430, Alpine, TX 79830
Web Address: www.our-town.com/stillwell

Hallie's Hall of Fame Museum near Big Bend National Park

The Life of Hallie Stillwell

Born in Waco on October 20, 1897, Hallie Crawford moved with her family when she was a year old to San Angelo. Her parents, constantly seeking better opportunities for the family and better education for the children, moved five times in twelve years—always in covered wagons. They finally settled in Alpine, Texas, in 1910.

In 1916 Hallie graduated from Alpine High School and got a teaching certificate from the Normal School for Teachers. Her first teaching job was in Presidio, a place her father thought too dangerous for his daughter. When he warned her she was on a wild goose chase, Hallie replied, "Then I'll gather my geese!" Years later she called her autobiography *I'll Gather My Geese*.

Ignoring her father's warning, Hallie armed herself with a six-shooter and headed for Presidio. She wore the gun every

Hallie Stillwell in a family photo in 1993.
Photo courtesy of the Stillwell Family

day, slogging a half-mile through sand to get to her school. It was a necessary precaution. Presidio was on the border in an area frequented by raiders and was a major crossing point for Pancho Villa. After a year there she took a job in Marathon. It was safer there, but Hallie didn't like it as much until she met a handsome cowboy named Roy Stillwell through mutual friends.

She soon fell in love, however her parents objected to the match: Stilwell was twenty years older than Hallie; he drank; he gambled. But Hallie said he "made my heart do flip-flops." She eloped with him on July 29, 1918. She was twenty. He was forty.

He took her home to Stillwell Ranch and a tiny one-room building that would be her home for many years. The three ranch hands were not pleased at the introduction of a woman into their lives. For starters, they had to start sleeping in the barn. Then she went and cleaned the coffee pot that they had perfectly seasoned. They complained for six months after-wards that the coffee was not fit to drink.

But Hallie slowly won them over. She was a better shot than any of them, and that gained their respect. She learned to herd cattle and brand calves, and she often shot game for their dinner. Once she shot a menacing puma.

The Stillwells had three children—Roy, Guy, and Dadie—and when they became school age, Hallie lived with them at the family home in town. But on weekends and summers, they all went back to the ranch. Through the years she mastered many skills to earn income for her family, among them barbering and candle making.

She was widowed in 1948 but continued living and working at the ranch until 1964. That year she moved into Marathon and became justice of the peace and coroner for Brewster County, leaving the ranch in the care of her sons.

In 1966 Hallie was a judge at the town's first chili cook-off. For the next four years she was elected Chili Cook-off Queen, an honor that she held until her death. By the time she opened Hallie's Hall of Fame in 1991, she had become a true Texas character and received honors from scores of organizations. She was inducted into the Cowgirl Hall of Fame in 1992, and into the Texas Women's Hall of Fame in 1994.

Hallie died in an Alpine hospital on August 18, 1997, two months and two days shy of her 100th birthday.

· Ladies of Letters ·

Some women made their marks quite literally—by putting pen to paper. **Dilue Rose Harris** was a pioneer, not a professional writer, but her recollections of the Texas Revolution became a classic source for historians. **Katherine Anne Porter** and **Sarah McClendon**, on the other hand, were professionals: Katherine won a Pulitzer Prize for fiction, and Sarah McClendon became a barrier-breaking journalist. **Sallie Reynolds Matthews** was a professional rancher, but her memoir offers a fascinating look at turn-of-the-century ranch life in Texas.

Dilue Rose Harris Site

The **Dilue Rose Harris House Museum** is in a home where Dilue once lived and probably wrote at least part of her book.

Hours: By appointment only (prefers groups of at least 25)
Admission: $2
Location: In central Columbus. From Highway 90, turn south onto Milam Street then left onto Washington Street. The museum is one block down, just past the intersection with Bowie Street.
Phone Number: 877-444-7339 (No direct line to the museum. This is a toll free number for the Convention & Visitors Bureau, which can set up a tour.)
Address: 602 Washington Street, Columbus, TX 78934
Web Address: www.columbustexas.org/musatr2.htm (This is the Columbus Convention & Visitors Bureau site, but it has information about the museum.)

The Dilue Rose Harris House in Columbus

Dilue is buried next to her husband, Ira, in the **Columbus City Cemetery**, which is off Highway 90 about a mile west of the Stafford Opera House.

The Life of Dilue Rose Harris

Dilue Rose was born on April 28, 1825, in St. Louis, Missouri, to Dr. Pleasant W. Rose and his wife, Margaret Wells Rose. The family moved to Texas in 1833, living first in Harrisburg then at Stafford's Point. Texas would soon be embroiled in a revolution against Mexico, and Dilue would be right there in the middle of it all.

Years later, toward the end of her long life, she wrote an account of the Texas Revolution based on her own recollections, interviews with others who lived through it, and her father's diary.

Of October 1835, she wrote, "The convention met at San Felipe in October. The first act was a call for volunteers to capture San Antonio before it could be reinforced by General Cos. Our school closed in September. The teacher said there was so much excitement that it affected the small children, and the young men could not be got back in school at all after the election in September. There was a constant talk of war."

After Texas won its independence, the Rose family moved to an area near Houston. On February 20, 1840, thirteen-year-old Dilue married Ira A. Harris, a New Yorker nine years her senior who served with the Texas Rangers. The Harris family lived in Houston until 1845, then they moved to Columbus. By 1858 they had built a cozy two-room home that they shared with their nine children. (That house is preserved today as the Dilue Rose Harris House Museum.)

Dilue was widowed in 1869. She never remarried. Thirty years later, when she was seventy-four years old, Dilue decided to write down her experiences during the Texas Revolution. Her chronicle was published in the *Quarterly of the Texas State Historical Association* and in the *Eagle Lake Headlight*.

Dilue died at Eagle Lake on April 2, 1914. She was eighty-nine.

Katherine Anne Porter Sites

The writer's hometown is proud of its famous daughter and has preserved her childhood home as **The Katherine Anne Porter Literary Center**. It includes a small museum. Southwest Texas State University leases the facility for its writer-in-residence program. The student who lives there acts as caretaker and gives programs in the community. During the fall and spring semesters, the Center hosts literary events that are

The Katherine Anne Porter Literacy Center in Kyle

open to the community. Recent participants include Pulitzer Prize winners Annie Proulx and Phillip Levine.

> *Hours*: 2 to 5 P.M. Sundays for the museum. Call or check the web site for literary events. Closed during the summer.
>
> *Admission*: Free
>
> *Location*: In Kyle, Texas. From Interstate 35, take exit 213 and merge onto I-35 S. Business/U.S. 81 South. There will be a stop sign at Center Street. Turn right and drive through town, past the First Baptist Church. The house is on the right between North Sledge and Gross Street.
>
> *Phone Number*: 512-268-6637
>
> *Address*: 508 West Center Street, Kyle, TX 78640
>
> *Web Address*: www.english.swt.edu/KAP/Default.html

There is also a **historical marker** in Kyle dedicated to Katherine on Center Street where it intersects with Burleson Street.

Katherine's ashes are buried next to her mother in **Indian Creek Cemetery** in Brownwood, Texas. The cemetery is on State Highway 377, ten miles south of the town.

The Life of Katherine Anne Porter

When little Callie Russell Porter announced at age six that she planned to be a writer, her family scoffed. Girls did not have careers outside the home, not in Texas at the end of the 1800s. But times were changing.

The girl grew up to win the Pulitzer Prize and National Book Award as Katherine Anne Porter.

She was born May 15, 1890, in Indian Creek, Texas. Two years later she lost her mother in childbirth. She moved, along with her father and three siblings, into her paternal grandmother's house in Kyle.

Grandma Cat (short for Catherine) provided the only stable home that young Callie would ever know. The old woman was stern and domineering, but she also delighted in telling stories and passed on that trait to her granddaughter.

Callie lived in Kyle until 1901, the year her grandmother died. Afterward her family moved to San Antonio. Her father was capricious and, by some accounts, abusive. And the family was poor, a source of embarrassment for the teenaged Callie.

To escape her family, she married a railroad clerk named John Henry Koontz when she was sixteen. The marriage lasted less than nine years. In divorce papers filed in 1915, Callie claims Koontz was abusive.

It was at about this time that Callie changed her name to Katherine Anne, in honor of her grandmother.

She spent the two years after her divorce recuperating from a bout with tuberculosis. Through a fellow patient she got a job in 1917 as a journalist for the Fort Worth newspaper the *Critic*. The following year she took a job as critic with the *Rocky*

Mountain News in Denver. She contracted influenza there and nearly died, an experience she later fictionalized in *Pale Horse, Pale Rider*.

In 1919 she moved to New York City and supported herself with odd jobs while writing magazine articles and short fiction. Beautiful, quixotic, and opinionated, Katherine loved to have a good time and had an active social life. She married again in 1926 to a man ten years her junior. That union ended in divorce after Katherine contracted gonorrhea. The infection ultimately necessitated a hysterectomy and ended Katherine's dreams of having a child.

In 1930 Katherine published a book of critically acclaimed short stories and started the novel *Ship of Fools*. She won a Guggenheim Fellowship the next year and went to work in Europe for a time. While there, she married again, this time to a novice writer thirteen years her junior. She divorced him in 1938 and promptly married a student who was twenty years younger than she. He was, reportedly, horrified when he discovered Katherine's true age, and the marriage was short lived. It would be Katherine's last. She didn't give up on men; she just stopped marrying them.

By the time of her fourth divorce, she was a bona fide literary star. Katherine took the post of first chair of poetry at the Library of Congress in Washington, D.C. in 1943. Then in 1945 she fled a soured relationship by taking a scriptwriting job in Hollywood. She stayed in California for the next four years but kept the initial job only a matter of months. She loathed the constraints put on scriptwriters and described Hollywood denizens as vulgar.

She taught at universities and worked to finish *Ship of Fools*, which was finally published in 1962. It was a critical and popular hit. In 1966 she won both the Pulitzer Prize and the National Book Award for *The Collected Stories of Katherine Anne Porter*.

For the rest of her life, she continued to teach and write sporadically.

Katherine Anne Porter died on September 18, 1980, at the age of ninety and was cremated. Though she often spoke of her dislike for Texas, she left instructions that her ashes be returned to Indian Creek and buried beside her mother.

Sarah McClendon Site

Long before she made a name for herself as a feisty journalist in Washington, D.C., Sarah McClendon lived in what is now called the **Bonner-Whitaker-McClendon House**. She grew up in the ornate Victorian home, which is now restored as a museum. Many McClendon family artifacts (including Sarah's first manual typewriter) are on display. The tour guides are well informed and can usually be counted on for colorful stories about Sarah and her family.

The McClendon Home in Tyler

Hours: 10 A.M. to 4 P.M. Saturdays, 1 to 4 P.M. Sundays.
  Group tours can be arranged. (Note: A caretaker lives
  in the house and is usually happy to give an
  impromptu tour.)

Admission: $5 for anyone 12 or older, free for anyone
  younger than 12

Location: Along Tyler's Azalea Trail (this makes it a nice
  place to visit in the spring). From Highway 31, turn
  south onto Highway 69/Broadway Street. Turn right
  onto W. Houston Street. The house is a big ol' Victorian, painted dark yellow with green and red trim.

Phone Number: 903-592-3533

Address: 806 W. Houston Street, Tyler, TX

Web Address: None as of press time, but the staff plans to
  have one by the end of 2001.

The Life of Sarah McClendon

Sarah McClendon was just one of the nine children of Annie and
Sidney McClendon, but she grew up to become a singular presence in the Washington press corps.

The Tyler, Texas native was born July 8, 1911, in what is
now the library of the home she grew up in. She was an intelligent, active child and knew from an early age that she wanted to
do something exciting with her life.

At first that meant being a lawyer. Then an acquaintance
convinced her to attend the journalism school at the University
of Missouri instead. It was a decision she never regretted.

After graduation she worked in Texas as a reporter for ten
years. When the United States entered World War II, Sarah
wanted to help. She wanted to be a spy. Instead, she joined the
Women's Army Corps in 1942 and was assigned the job of public affairs officer.

She was soon transferred to the WAC in Washington, D.C.,
a post she has described as "interesting as can be." Two years
later she became pregnant and was discharged from the WAC.

However she was not without a job. In June of 1944—the month she was forced out of the Army—the *Philadelphia Daily News* hired her to be its Washington correspondent.

Sarah got her first White House press pass and began covering the administration of Franklin D. Roosevelt. She was thrilled—and terrified. Decades later she joked that she didn't start asking questions until the Truman Administration. She has covered every presidential administration since then (up to George W. Bush in 2001, as of press time).

Along the way, she earned a reputation for dogged reporting and asking direct questions. Rumor has it that Lyndon Johnson asked more than one newspaper to take her off the White House beat. She was the first woman admitted to the National Press Club.

Sarah worked for a number of papers before becoming a freelance journalist. In 1997, at the age of eighty-six, she was still writing a weekly newspaper column, doing a weekly radio commentary, and putting out a biweekly newsletter.

Encroaching poor health made her cut back on her schedule, but as this book was being completed in the spring of 2001, she was still working and rarely missed a day at the White House.

When asked about retiring, she often responds with a story about someone who worked "on her deathbed."

Sallie Reynolds Matthews Site

Rancher/writer Sallie Reynolds Matthews gets a room to herself in the **Old Jail Art Center** in Albany, Texas. The restored 1877 building (it really was a jail) features displays of pre-Columbian artwork, an Asian collection that includes Chinese tomb figures, and works by American and European artists. But

Sally gets her own little room, featuring photos and artifacts related to her life.

Hours: 10 A.M. to 5 P.M. Tues.-Sat., 2 to 5 P.M. Sundays
    Closed major holidays
Admission: Free
Location: In Albany, just east of the Shackelford County
    Courthouse
Phone Number: 915-762-2269
Address: 201 South Second Street, Albany, TX 76430
Web Address: www.albanytexas.com/attractions/
    artcenter.html

The Life of Sallie Reynolds Matthews

Sallie Reynolds was born on the Cantrell Ranch on May 23, 1861, to Barber and Anne Marie Reynolds.

At fifteen she helped start a classic Texas tale by marrying John Alexander "Bud" Matthews on Christmas Day 1876 in a stone house by the Brazos River. Together, they had nine children. The last, Watkins "Watt" Reynolds Matthews, came along on February 1, 1899. The family ranch—and the ranchers—would soon be among the most famous in the state.

That was due in no small part to Sallie, who wrote about her life in *Interwoven: A Pioneer Chronicle*, which was published in 1936. The book is a favorite with historians looking to explore the late 1800s and early 1900s in West Texas: storms, hostile Indians, heat, isolation...all can be found in *Interwoven*.

Sallie, a longtime member of the National Cowgirl Hall of Fame, died on September 14, 1938, at the age of seventy-seven in Albany, Texas.

Sallie Reynolds Matthews
Photo courtesy of The UT Institute of Texan Cultures at San Antonio

· The Musically Inclined ·

Ask someone to use the words "Texas" and "music" in a sentence, and it is unlikely the name **Olga Samaroff** will come up. But it should, along with **Janis Joplin** and **Selena**. All three excelled in their musical endeavors: Olga as a classical pianist, Janis with rock, and of course Selena with tejano.

Olga Samaroff Site

Olga Samaroff lived in a pretty **Victorian house** at 2327 Avenue M when she was growing up in Galveston. It is a private home so there are no public tours, but it is easy to find for a quick look from the outside. From the seawall, turn onto 23rd Street then turn left onto Avenue M.

The Life of Olga Samaroff

Olga Samaroff was born Lucy Jane Olga Hickenlooper on August 8, 1882, in San Antonio. She moved with her family first to Houston, then to Galveston where they settled in the late 1880s. Olga attended the Ursuline Convent there.

She was a piano prodigy, and her mother and grandmother encouraged her abilities. Her grandmother had been a concert pianist in Europe. Olga moved to Paris with her grandmother in 1894. The following year she became the first American woman to win a scholarship at the prestigious Paris Conservatoire. She graduated in 1897 then continued her studies with renowned pianists.

To the dismay of her family, she put her studies aside around the turn of the century when she married a Russian civil servant named Boris Loutzky. They lived in St. Petersburg for

Olga Samaroff
Photo courtesy of The Rosenberg Library Galveston, Texas

three years, but Loutzky was abusive and Olga divorced him. She resumed her studies and planned her first tour.

She faced one final obstacle, however—her name. The prejudice against American artists was a career killer, so she changed her last name to Samaroff in 1904. Her tour was a success, and Olga soon became a respected classical pianist worldwide.

Illness forced her to take time off from touring in 1910. The following year she married conductor Leopold Stokowski, but they divorced in 1923. They had one daughter, Sonya Stokowski.

Before an arm injury ended her touring career in 1926, Olga became the first American woman pianist to present all thirty-two Beethoven sonatas in recital. She was also one of the first women pianists to make recordings. After the injury, Olga turned to teaching and writing about music for a living. She was the first American-born artist-teacher at the Juliard School of Music, and for many years she was the only American-born member of the piano faculty. In 1926 she became the first woman critic for a New York newspaper when she took the post of music critic at the *New York Evening Post*. Beginning in 1928 she chaired the piano department of the Philadelphia Conservatory in addition to her other work. She also published music books.

During the Great Depression she helped organize the Musicians' Emergency Aid and participated in a number of civic activities that promoted appreciation of music by laymen.

She died on May 17, 1948, in New York. Her students wrote a letter to the editor of the *New York Times* stating, "Her greatness as a musician was surpassed only by her greatness as a human being."

Janis Joplin Site

Janis' true legacy is in her music and the musicians she influenced, but to get a more material Janis experience, head to Port Arthur and the **Museum of the Gulf Coast**. The centerpiece of the exhibit is her famous car with its psychedelic paint job. There are also a statue, gold records, clothing, photos, and memorabilia from her childhood.

Hours: 9 A.M. to 5 P.M., Mon.-Sat., 1 to 5 P.M. Sundays
Admission: $3.50 adults, $3 senior citizens, $1.50 children
     6 to 18, 50 cents children younger than 6
Location: Second floor of the museum. To get to the
     museum, take Highway 69 south from Beaumont.
     Drive all the way through Port Arthur to Procter
     Street. Take a right and drive past Lamar State Col-
     lege. Turn left on Beaumont Avenue, then take the
     first left into the museum parking lot. It is across the
     street from the City of Port Arthur Police Department.
Phone Number: 409-982-7000
Address: 700 Procter, Port Arthur, TX 77640
Web Address: www.pa.lamar.edu/museum/gulf.html

The Life of Janis Joplin

Few Texans have ever achieved the name recognition that Janis Lyn Joplin built in just twenty-seven years.

She was born into a middle-class family on January 19, 1943, in Port Arthur. The rebelliousness that would make her an icon made its presence known in middle school. By the time Janis graduated from Jefferson High School in 1960, her class-mates had dubbed her a "slut," and she had a reputation for promiscuity and heavy drinking.

After a brief, unpleasant stint at the Lamar State College of Technology at Beaumont, Janis fled to Austin and the University of Texas where she studied art—but rarely did class work. Instead, she haunted the local music scene and even started

Janis Joplin as a young musician
Photo courtesy of the Museum of the Gulf Coast

Janis Joplin at the height of her success
Photo courtesy of the Museum of the Gulf Coast

singing a bit herself. One gig led to another and eventually to Threadgill's, a popular joint with the party crowd. It was there that she met Kenneth Threadgill, the bar's owner. He befriended her and urged her to keep singing.

In Texas Janis was a hippie in a square world. San Francisco was another world entirely. Janis moved there in 1963 and for the next two years built up a loyal local audience and a serious drug problem. When the drug addiction got so bad that she could no longer perform, friends bought her a bus ticket back to Texas. When she got home Janis weighed less than ninety pounds.

She got sober and healthy and considered her options—Port Arthur or San Francisco? San Francisco won when Janis got the chance to audition there with a band called Big Brother and the Holding Company. She got the gig.

Within a year she was a rising star; within two years she was a bona fide superstar; and within four years she was dead. Janis died October 5, 1970, of an accidental overdose of heroin and alcohol. Her ashes were scattered in San Francisco Bay.

Selena Sites

Corpus Christi brims with places that can evoke Selena's memory—restaurants where she ate, schools she attended... all the places she went in her hometown. Walk around the Molina neighborhood where she lived and talk with people: You're bound to find someone who knew her. Here's a rundown of some specific places to go to vicariously experience her life... and her death.

See Selena's costumes, her red Porsche, photographs, and memorabilia at the **Selena Museum** in the Q-Production recording studios. The tour includes a stop in a room where

Selena recorded many of her songs. Absolutely no cameras allowed.

Hours: 9 to 11:45 A.M. and 1 to 6 P.M. Mon.-Fri.
Admission: Free
Location: Inside the recording studio, which is between
    McBride Lane and the Leopard Street entrance to the
    Corpus Christi Greyhound Race Track
Phone Number: 361-289-9013
Address: 5410 Leopard Street, Corpus Christi, TX 78408
Web Address: www.q-productions.com/museum.htm

West Oso Junior High School at 1115 Bloomington St. Selena attended classes here but dropped out in the eighth grade. She later got an equivalency degree.

Take a walk down **Bloomington Street** in the Molina neighborhood. Selena lived with her family in a house at 709. After her marriage, Selena and her husband moved next door to 705. To find the neighborhood, exit Highway 358 at W. Point Road and turn east. Take a left onto Molina Drive. The family no longer lives there.

The city of Corpus Christi built a waterfront memorial to Selena and dubbed it **Mirador del Flor.** It's a large white pavilion with murals, an enormous sculpted white rose, and a statue of the slain singer. Because of vandalism, there are plans to add a barrier to the memorial to keep destructive folks at bay. To get to it from Interstate 37, follow the signs to Shoreline Boulevard and turn right. The monument is where Shoreline crosses Peoples Street. It's hard to miss.

The singer's Grammy-winning *Selena Live* was recorded in **Memorial Coliseum** in February 1993. The coliseum is near Mirador del Flor, at 402 S. Shoreline Boulevard.

Selena opened her first boutique, **Selena, Etc.**, at 4926 Everhart Road in 1994. Her sister now runs the shop. You can exit onto Everhart from Highway 358. Turn north. The shop is on the left.

Mirador del Flor—The Selena memorial in Corpus Christi

A former employee fatally shot Selena in one of the rooms of the **Corpus Christi-Days Inn Airport.** From Corpus Christi International Airport, go east onto Highway 44. At the intersection with Highway 358, turn left. Where it intersects with I-37, turn right and proceed east until you reach Exit 3-A. This is Navigation Boulevard. Exit and turn right. The hotel is on the right.

Selena was buried in **Seaside Memorial Cemetery.** From downtown Corpus Christi, drive south on Shoreline. Just past the Bay Shore Inn there is a sign for Seaside Memorial Park and Funeral Home. Turn right. (If you're still on Shoreline and you pass the Sea Ranch Motel, you've gone too far.) Once inside the cemetery, follow the road as it curves past a monument inscribed with "FOR THE LAMB SHALL LEAD THEM." Turn left there. Head towards a large monument showing Christ on the cross. Follow the road as it curves by that monument and past it for about one-tenth of a mile. You will see a flagpole on the left. Selena's grave is across the road from it.

The Life of Selena Quintanilla Perez

Selena Quintanilla was born into a Mexican-American family on April 16, 1971, in Lake Jackson, Texas, where the family owned a restaurant called Pappagallo.

Her father had performed with a tejano band for almost twenty years, and he passed his skills and love for music to his children. When Selena was eight years old, her family began performing together as a band called Los Dinos, at the family restaurant and at local weddings. At that time Selena spoke only English, so she had to learn Spanish to perform with the group.

After two years the group—now called Selena y Los Dinos—turned pro and the year after that moved to Corpus Christi where the family continued to perform together. Under the tutelage of her father, Abraham Quintanilla, Selena kept a punishing touring schedule and began appearing on Spanish-language television shows. Eventually, she missed so much school that she dropped out in the eighth grade. (She later got an equivalency degree.)

Selena's lovely voice and flamboyant style soon earned her and Los Dinos a following in the United States and in Mexico. In 1987, when she was just sixteen years old, Selena won the Tejano Music Award for Female Entertainer of the Year. She had been recording with small tejano labels, but in 1989 she got a six-figure contract with EMI Latin Records. By that time she was commonly called "the queen of tejano."

In 1992 she began her own clothing line, and she became the first tejana singer to sell more than 300,000 albums with *Entre a Mi Mundo*.

The same year, she defied her father and eloped with Los Dinos guitarist Christopher Perez on April 2.

Selena y Los Dinos won a Grammy Award in 1993 for *Selena Live!* and the group began to cross over from the tejano scene into the mainstream. In 1994 *Texas Monthly* chose Selena for its annual issue on twenty influential Texans, and *Hispanic* magazine reported her net worth at $5 million.

She also opened Selena, Etc. boutiques in Corpus Christi and San Antonio that year.

At the 1995 Houston Livestock Show and Rodeo, Selena y Los Dinos attracted 61,041 people, more than country music superstars Clint Black, George Strait, and Reba McEntire.

Selena was on the verge of mainstream stardom when she was shot to death by Yolanda Saldivar, a former employee and fan club president. She was twenty-four years old when she died on March 31, 1995. Her first bilingual album, *Dreaming of You*, was released four months later and hit number one on the national *Billboard* Top 200 in its first week.

Selena's death triggered enormous grief for her fans, and many of them compared the event to the deaths of John Lennon and Elvis Presley. More than 30,000 people viewed her casket

Selena

Photo courtesy The UT Institute of Texan Cultures at San Antonio,
The San Antonio Light Collection.
(Photograph by Ric Vasquez)

at the Bayfront Plaza Convention Center in Corpus Christi before her funeral.

She is credited with bringing tejano music to the attention of mainstream audiences and is remembered both for her music and her style.

· Artful Daubers ·

Though neither was a Texas native, sculptor **Elizabet Ney** and painter **Georgia O'Keeffe** did significant work while living in Texas.

Elizabet Ney Sites

The **Elizabet Ney Museum** in Austin preserves the artist's castle-like studio and displays personal memorabilia along with the largest single collection of her work. Children's programs are offered in the summer.

Hours: 10 A.M. to 5 P.M. Wed.-Sat., noon to 5 P.M. Sundays
Admission: Free
Location: North central Austin. From Interstate 35, take the exit for 45th Street and go northwest to Avenue H. Turn left. The museum is one block up at the intersection with 44th Street.
Phone Number: 512-458-2255
Address: 302 E. 44th Street, Austin, TX 78751
Web Address: www.austincityguide.com/ads/elizabetney/ main_si.htm

Check out the artist's famous **sculpture of Stephen F. Austin** in the Texas State Capitol Building. (See the Capital Women chapter for more information.)

Elizabet is buried at **Liendo Plantation** in Hempstead, where she lived from 1873 to 1907.

Hours: Open for public tours on the first Saturday of most
    months. Tours begin at 10 A.M., 11:30 A.M., and 1 P.M.
    Private group tours available
Admission: $7 adults, $5 students and senior citizens
    Group rates available
Location: From Houston, take Highway 290 west toward
    Hempstead and take the exit for FM 1488. Turn right
    and drive for about a mile and half to Wyatt Chapel
    Road. It is the first paved road on the right. Turn
    right. The plantation is about a mile down on the
    right. (If driving south on Interstate 45, take FM 1488
    exit off the freeway and go west toward Hempstead.)
Phone Number: 979-826-3126
Address: Route 4 Box 386, Hempstead, TX 77445
Web Address: www.liendo.org/plantat.html

The Life of Elizabet Ney

Elizabet Ney was an art pioneer in Texas.

Born in Muenster, Germany, on January 26, 1833, she
showed a talent for art early in her life. Her father was an artist,
but Elizabet's family frowned on a woman following that path.
Incensed, Elizabeth refused to eat until they came around.
Frustrated, they called in a family friend—a bishop—to inter-
vene. He was so impressed with Elizabet's talent and
determination that he persuaded her family to let her have her
way. Subsequently, she became the first woman sculpture student accepted at the Munich Art Academy.

During a visit with a friend in Heidelberg, the young artist
fell in love with a Scottish doctor named Edmund Montgomery.
They married, but Elizabet never changed her last name—a
fact that scandalized the community and led to gossip that she
was actually Montgomery's mistress.

In the early 1870s the couple decided to move to the United
States. After a few years in Georgia, they moved to Texas in
1873, where they would live the rest of their lives. First they

Elisabet Ney painting in her studio.
Photo courtesy of The UT Institute of Texan Cultures at San Antonio

bought a farm near Hempstead and called it Liendo. For the next two decades, Elizabet's career stagnated as she concentrated on home life.

She began sculpting seriously again in the early 1890s. In 1892 she was commissioned to do sculptures of Texas heroes Sam Houston and Stephen F. Austin for the Chicago World's Fair. The statue of Austin is now in the Texas State Capitol Building.

Elizabet built a second home and art studio in Austin, dubbing it Formosa. She continued to live at Liendo and commuted to the studio, where she worked steadily until her death in 1907. Elizabet was buried at Liendo.

Georgia O'Keeffe Sites

Georgia is most readily associated with New Mexico, but she spent several years in West Texas early in her career, and there are a number of interesting places there associated with her.

The **Panhandle Plains Museum** in Canyon has one of the only oil paintings done by the artist, who primarily worked with watercolors. The museum is on the grounds of West Texas A&M University, which was called West Texas Normal College when she taught there.

Hours: 9 A.M. to 5 P.M. Mon.-Sat. 1 to 6 P.M. Sundays June-August open until 6 P.M. Mon.-Sat.

Admission: $4 adults and children older than 12, $3 senior citizens, $1 children 4 to 12, children younger than 4 get in free. Group rates available. Admission on Sundays is free. Closed major holidays.

Location: On the campus of West Texas A&M University. From Interstate 40 in Amarillo, take Interstate 27 south to Canyon. (There's a lot of construction around

I-40 in Amarillo, so watch carefully for the exit.) Watch for U.S. 87 and follow the signs for it when it splits with I-27. It will take you all the way into Canyon. Turn left onto Fourth Avenue. Note: Fourth Avenue is also State Highway 217. The museum will be on your left. Parking is across the street.

Phone Number: 806-651-2244
Address: 2401 Fourth Avenue, Canyon, TX 79016
Web Address: www.wtamu.edu/museum

When she first arrived in Canyon, Georgia stayed at a boarding house run by Mary Hudspeth. She reportedly disliked the décor because it was too frilly. However, after she moved out she continued to take many of her meals there. Andrea and Todd Stephens recently bought the house and turned it into a bed-and-breakfast called **Hudspeth House**. (Georgia probably would hate the décor.) The service is a bit hit and miss—guests with reservations have been known to arrive to a locked, empty house, and breakfast choices are limited. But when you can find them, the Stephens are cheerful, helpful hosts.

Hours: Vary
Admission: Prices vary. Check Web site or call for up-to-date rates.
Location: In Canyon's historic district, just down the street from West Texas A&M University
Phone Number: 800-655-9809 or 806-655-9800
Address: 1905 Fourth Avenue, Canyon, TX 79015
Web Address: www.hudspethinn.com

The home where Georgia lived most of her time in Canyon, now called **The Shirley House**, is just a few blocks from the Hudspeth House at the northwest corner of 5th and 20th Streets. It is a private residence, and the owner does not welcome tourists.

Don't miss **Palo Duro Canyon**, a frequent subject of Georgia's. She loved its wild beauty and painted it frequently. To get there from Amarillo, head south on Interstate 27, then take FM 1062 east.

In Amarillo, the **Amarillo Museum of Art** has three Georgia O'Keeffe watercolors.

Hours: 10 A.M. to 5 P.M. Tues.-Fri., 1 to 5 P.M. Sat.-Sun.
  Closed major holidays
Admission: Free
Location: On the northeast corner of the Amarillo College Washington Street campus. From I-40, take the Washington Street exit and go south on Washington Street. Turn left onto W. 22nd Street. The museum is at the intersection of W. 22nd Street and S. Van Buren.
Phone Number: 806-371-5050
Address: 2200 S. Van Buren, Amarillo, TX 79109
Web Address: www.amarilloart.org

The Life of Georgia O'Keeffe

Georgia O'Keeffe was born in Wisconsin on November 15, 1887, the first of seven children for Francis and Ida O'Keeffe. The family lived in Wisconsin and Virginia during her childhood, and education was emphasized for all the children, boys and girls.

Georgia knew by the time she was in eighth grade that she wanted to be an artist. In addition to her formal schooling, Georgia consistently took private art classes.

In 1905 she enrolled at the Art Institute of Chicago, but she contracted typhoid fever and did not return the following year. In 1907 she enrolled in the Art Students League in New York City and there she was awarded the Chase Still Life Scholarship. She was unhappy with her work and for a year or so, abandoned it. She worked for a time as a commercial artist in Chicago until, disillusioned with art as a career, she quit and moved back to Virginia where she enrolled in classes at the University of Virginia.

A teacher introduced her to new artistic methods in the summer of 1912, and Georgia's desire for a career in the arts burgeoned again.

She visited Texas for the first time in 1912, drawn by a sense of adventure and a desire to teach art herself. She later said that she was overwhelmed by the dry, open landscape and "the beauty of that wild world."

Georgia was supervisor of art for the Amarillo public schools for two years; however, she clashed with the school board over salary and the cost of textbooks, and her contract was terminated in 1914.

Looking to continue her own education, she attended Columbia University in New York City. During the summers she taught at the University of Virginia. Texas called again in 1916, and she took a job at West Texas State Normal College in Canyon. At about this same time, she earned a fan in New York art gallery owner Alfred Stieglitz. He displayed her charcoals, and his support bolstered her reputation in the art world and with her students.

While in Texas, Georgia created at least fifty paintings—oils and watercolors inspired by the landscape. In 1918 she took sick leave from the college and never returned. After recuperating, she returned to New York at the urging of Stieglitz who had fallen in love with her. He was still married but separated from his wife, and he and Georgia began an affair. They lived together until 1924, when Stieglitz's wife divorced him. Georgia was indifferent to marriage, but Stieglitz was adamant and they married on December 11 of that year. By that time Georgia was considered one of the top artists of her time.

Restless after years in the northeast, Georgia longed for an adventure and set out in 1928 with a friend for a trip to New Mexico. Enraptured, she began yearly visits to New Mexico, dubbing it "the faraway."

In 1940 she bought a studio near Abiquiu, New Mexico, but continued to commute between New Mexico and New York City. She bought a house in Abiquiu and moved there full time after her husband died in 1946.

Wildly popular for decades, Georgia's art fell from favor in the 1950s. She kept painting but had only three solo shows. She spent time at her home in New Mexico and traveling the world.

In 1962 she was elected to American Academy of Arts and Letters, and in the 1970s the public rediscovered her work and she became more popular than ever. She stopped painting in 1972 as her eyesight failed, but she took up the brush again the following year. President Gerald Ford awarded her the nation's highest civilian honor, the Medal of Freedom, in 1977. In 1984, with her health failing, Georgia moved to Santa Fe. She died there on March 6, 1986, in St. Vincent Hospital at the age of ninety-eight. After she was cremated the next day, her long-time friend and business manager, Juan Hamilton, took her ashes to the top of Pedernal Mountain and scattered them in the wind.

· The Ultimate Philanthropist ·

Ima Hogg Sites

Now let's get this straight—there was no Ura Hogg. There was only Ima, who became a patron of the arts, champion of historic preservation, and generous philanthropist. East Texas teems with places that have an Ima connection.

The house where she was born in **Mineola** has been torn down, but Douglas and Margaret Hoke bought the property, lobbied to get a historical marker for the site, and created an amazingly lovely landscaped area complete with benches, bowers, and a fishpond. They welcome visitors to the site, and it is not unusual to find people picnicking there or taking pictures. The Hokes live next door in the O.P. Pyle House, and they're usually quite receptive to strangers with questions about Ima Hogg. To get there, turn north onto Line Street from Highway 80 in Mineola. The O.P. Pyle house is number 123 and the Ima Hogg birthplace is next to it.

The **Governor Hogg Shrine State Historical Park** is a tiny park complex in Quitman. It has the home where Ima's parents spent the early years of their marriage and a museum named in honor of Ima Hogg that includes a small display about her.

Hours: 9 A.M. to noon and 1 to 4 P.M. seven days a week
  Closed on major holidays
Admission: Free
Location: In the middle of Quitman, just off Highway 37
  across the street from an insurance agency.
Phone Number: 903-763-2701

Address: 101 Governor Hogg Parkway, Quitman, TX
    75783
Web Address: www.tpwd.state.tx.us/park/govhogg

Douglas and Margaret Hoke in the garden they
have created at Ima Hogg's birthplace in Mineola.

Varner-Hogg Plantation State Historical Park is a sixty-five-acre tract with a lovely, completely furnished antebellum mansion once owned by the Hogg family. Ima donated the property to the state in 1957. Tour guides are knowledgeable and have lots of stories to tell about "Miss Ima."

Hours: 9 to 11 A.M. and 1 to 4 P.M., Wed.-Sat., 1 to 4 P.M.
    Sundays
Admission: $4 adults, $2 students, Free for children younger than 6
Location: Two miles north of West Columbia on FM 2852.
    From Houston, take State Highway 288 south to State
    Highway 35. Turn south on State Highway 35 and

travel 12 miles to West Columbia. Outside West Columbia take FM 2852 to Park Road 51 (1702 North 13th Street).
Phone Number: 979-345-4656
Address: Box 696, West Columbia, TX 77486
Web Address: www.tpwd.state.tx.us/park/varner/

Varner-Hogg Plantation Manor at Varner-Hogg State Park
Photo courtesy of Varner-Hogg State Park

By far the best of the Ima Hogg sites is **Bayou Bend**. She lived in this mansion for much of her adult life and designed its gardens as outdoor living spaces. She donated the property to Houston's Museum of Fine Art in 1957 but continued living there until 1965. The site opened as a museum in 1966 and houses Miss Ima's collection of American decorative arts as well as Hogg family memorabilia. Guided and self-guided tours of the house and magnificent gardens are available, and special arrangements can be made for tours. Cameras, packages, and handbags must be checked during all tours.

Hours: 1 to 5 P.M. Sat.-Sun. Last admission at 4 P.M. for
self-guided tours of the home. 10 to 11:30 A.M. and 1
to 2:45 P.M. Tues.-Fri. and 10 to 11:15 A.M. Saturdays
for guided tours of the home. 10 A.M. to 5 P.M.
Tues.-Sat. for self-guided tours of the gardens. 10 to
11 A.M. Tuesdays and Fridays for guided tours of the
gardens. Note: Reservations are required for all
guided tours.

Admission: $10 adults, $8.50 senior citizens and students
with ID, $5 children ages 10-18, $1.50 children younger than 10.

Location: West of downtown Houston, inside the 610
Loop, just south of Interstate 10. Take the Westcott
Street exit off I-10. (From Memorial Drive, turn south
at Westcott and park in the free public lot. Cross the
footbridge to the Jones Visitors Center.)

Phone Number: 713-639-7750

Address: One Westcott Street, Houston, TX 77007

Web Address: www.bayoubend.uh.edu/

She was buried in the family plot in **Oakwood Cemetery** in
Austin, 1601 Navasota Street. The cemetery is directly across
Interstate 35 from the University of Texas main campus.

The Life of Ima Hogg

Ima Hogg was born July 10, 1882, in Mineola, Texas, to Sarah
Ann Stinson Hogg and James Stephen Hogg. She was the second of their four children, the only daughter, and came by her
unfortunate name through family connections: "Ima" was the
name of the heroine in an epic poem about the Civil War written
by her uncle.

She was playing piano by the time she was three years old
and was always encouraged by her family to pursue music.
When she was eight Ima's father was elected governor of
Texas, and the family moved to Austin.

Ima's mother was frail and unwell much of the time, so Ima often accompanied her father to civic meetings and on trips—both while he was governor and afterward. Ima grew up mostly in Austin and began her studies at the University of Texas in 1899. In 1901 she went to New York to study music. Six years later she went to Europe for further study, spending 1907 through 1909 primarily in Vienna and Berlin.

Afterward she moved to Houston where she helped found the Houston Symphony Orchestra. She later served as its president. She also started giving piano lessons to a small number of students. Late in 1918 Ima became ill and went to Philadelphia where she spent the next two years under the care of a specialist in mental and nervous disorders. She finally returned to Houston in 1923.

While she was gone, oil was found on Hogg property in West Columbia, making the already well-to-do family quite rich. When Miss Ima returned to Houston she put the money to good use, donating funds to a variety of causes including the Houston Child Guidance Center. Her brother, Will, died in 1930, and with money he left, Ima established the Hogg Foundation for Mental Hygiene.

In 1943 Miss Ima, a Democrat like her father, was elected to the Houston school board. She fought to establish equal pay for teachers regardless of their gender or race. She also championed music programs for children in the public schools.

In 1948 she became the first woman president of the Philosophical Society of Texas.

In the 1950s Miss Ima gave away her family homes. After restoring the plantation in West Columbia, she donated it to the state of Texas in 1957. It is now Varner-Hogg Plantation State Historical Site. The same year, she gave Houston's Museum of Fine Art her Bayou Bend mansion and her extensive collection of American decorative arts. However, she continued living on the Houston estate until 1965 while it was converted from a private home into a museum. It opened to the public in 1966.

Miss Ima continued her historic preservation efforts in the 1960s by restoring a nineteenth-century stagecoach stop at Round Top called the Winedale Inn. She donated it to the University of Texas. She also saved her parents' old home in Quitman and donated it to the state as well. She won an award for "meritorious service in historic preservation" from the Texas Historical Commission in 1967. Two years later the town of Quitman established the Ima Hogg Museum in her honor. Both structures are now part of the Governor Hogg Shrine State Historical Park.

Throughout the 1970s Miss Ima was showered with awards for her work with the arts and charitable causes. She died after a traffic accident in London on August 19, 1975, at the age of ninety-three. After a funeral at Bayou Bend, she was buried in the Hogg family plot in Oakwood Cemetery in Austin.

· Medicine Women ·

Frances "Daisy" Allen and **May Owen** were medical pioneers who opened the doors of their profession so other women could walk through.

May Owen Site

The Physiology Hall of the **Museum of Science and History** in Fort Worth is dedicated to Dr. May Owen, who was instrumental in bringing the original Hall of Health Sciences into existence.

> *Hours*: 9 A.M. to 5 P.M. Mon.-Thurs., 9 A.M. to 8 P.M.,
>   Fri.-Sat., noon to 5:30 P.M. Sundays
> *Admission*: $6.50 adult, $5.50 senior citizen, $4.50 junior
> *Location*: One mile north of I-30 in Fort Worth's Cultural
>   District
> *Phone Number*: 817-255-9300 or 888-255-9300
> *Address*: 1501 Montgomery Street, Fort Worth, TX 76107
> *Web Address*: www.fwmuseum.org/geninfo.html

The Life of May Owen

May Owen was a farm girl from Falls County who didn't even get to attend high school until she was twenty-one years old, but she became the state's leading pathologist and a pioneer for women in medicine.

She was the first woman accepted at her medical school and the first woman president of the Texas Medical Association. At age nine, when she first voiced her desire to become a doctor, her only aim was to help people. She wanted to be like the doctor who frequently visited her ailing mother. Her father dismissed the notion as foolishness and told her never to mention it again.

Born May 3, 1891, May was the sixth of eight children. She contracted polio when she was still an infant, but the illness was not diagnosed until years later when May herself figured out that she had had the disease.

After her mother died, May took on increasing amounts of work on the family farm while pursuing as much schooling as she could get. When she was thirteen she completed seventh grade and had no way to finish her education. The nearest high school was more than ten miles away, and May was needed on the farm.

Her eldest brother came to her rescue eight years later when he arranged for her to attend high school in Fort Worth. She was twenty-one and had to support herself while attending classes, but she graduated top of her class in 1913 and earned a scholarship to Texas Christian University. While attending college, she worked as a laboratory technician.

In 1917 she graduated from TCU with a bachelor of arts degree. After graduation she continued to work as a laboratory technician while casting about for a medical school that would accept her. She was delighted when Louisville Medical School accepted her, though she did not know at the time that she was its first woman student—or that the male students had marched to the dean's office to protest that fact.

While she was attending medical school, the flu epidemic of 1918 swept the country and May decided to become a pathologist so she could find cures for such diseases. By the time she graduated in 1921, she had won over most of her male classmates and received a standing ovation when she received her diploma.

She did further training at the Mayo Clinic and Bellevue Hospital in New York City, where she worked crime scenes and performed autopsies on crime victims.

Returning to Fort Worth, she went to work for Terrell Laboratories and consulted with hospitals, often putting in sixteen-hour days, seven days a week. In 1935 she was called to consult on a case that would lead to fame for her in the scientific community. A teenager who had had a successful appendectomy continued to suffer from vomiting, cramps, and nausea more than a year after the procedure. May discovered that the powder used in surgical gloves could cause scarring, adhesions, and peritonitis.

May had made a name for herself and, more to the point, surgeons stopped using the dangerous glove powder. TCU awarded her an honorary doctor of science degree for the discovery in 1936.

May received scores of awards and honors during her lifetime, including the Texas Medical Association's highest honor, the Distinguished Service Award. In 1960 she became the first woman elected president of that organization. She was instrumental in setting up a revolving fund, the May Owen Irrevocable Trust, to provide financial help to students pursuing medical careers.

A series of falls and increasingly poor health kept her out of her office more than she liked toward the end of her life. But she did literally work until the day she died, at the age of ninety-seven, succumbing to a heart attack on April 12, 1988, after a full workday on April 11.

Frances "Daisy" Allen Site

A **historical marker** at 301 Fifth Street in Fort Worth shows where the Fort Worth Medical College once stood. Inscribed on it is "Among those in its small charter class was Frances Daisy Emery, the First Woman Medical School Graduate in Texas."

The Life of Frances Allen

Frances Emery, who always went by "Daisy," was born September 5, 1876, and knew she wanted to be a doctor by the time she was four years old. Flouting the traditions of the times, her schoolteacher father was a strong supporter of this idea.

Daisy was living with her family in Fort Worth when the Fort Worth Medical College opened. Her application was rejected, but legend has it that the school trustees reconsidered when she pointed out that the school rules did not specifically exclude women. She started classes with the school's first class in 1894.

Three years later she became the first woman to graduate from medical school in Texas. Of the event, the *Fort Worth Gazette* reported, "Among the graduates in the front row of seats appeared a bright winsome little woman, a fair Minerva whose presence in the class was a feature of unusual interest."

After a brief stint in private practice, she went to Washington, D.C. to complete a residency and internship at Women and Children's Medical Center. While there, Daisy had the opportunity to attend lectures by the era's feminist leaders—among them, Elizabeth Cady Stanton and Susan B. Anthony. Daisy even made herself a pair of bloomers. Her abolitionist father had instilled in her a strong sense of social justice that she would carry with her throughout life.

Daisy returned to Texas in 1901, went back into private practice, and taught at Dallas Medical College. In 1903 she married a medical school classmate, James Allen, and they started a joint practice and had two daughters.

When Daisy was widowed unexpectedly in 1913, she returned to Fort Worth but refused the offers from family members who invited her to live with them. Instead, she opened a private practice and taught at Fort Worth University. The school closed in 1917, but her private practice flourished, thanks to word of mouth among the women who were her patients.

Remembering the lessons of her father, she treated the poor for free and became active in the League of Women Voters.

Daisy retired in 1950, when she was seventy-four years old, but she continued to see a few longtime patients. She died on December 7, 1958.

· Texas's Yellow Rose ·

Myth or Heroine of the Revolution?

Was there a Yellow Rose of Texas? The experts can't agree, but she's mighty famous whether she existed or not.

The Yellow Rose of Texas Site

If the Yellow Rose was real, she gained her fame at the Battle of San Jacinto. If she's not, that's where the legend started. Either way, it's worth a look at the **San Jacinto Monument and Museum**. Considering the legend, this most phallic of monuments is the perfect way to remember the Yellow Rose.

> *Hours*: 9 A.M. to 6 P.M. daily
> *Admission*: Free
> *Location*: Twenty miles east of downtown Houston. From Loop 610, take Texas Highway 225 East for eight miles. Exit on Battleground Road and turn left.
> *Phone Number*: 281-479-2421
> *Address*: One Monument Circle, La Porte, Texas 77571-9744
> *Web Address*: www.neosoft.com/~sjm/hours.html

The Legend of the Yellow Rose of Texas

According to legend, the Yellow Rose was a young servant girl who dallied with Santa Anna in 1836, giving Sam Houston's troops the opportunity to catch the Mexican commander with his pants down—quite literally, if the story is true.

The San Jacinto Monument
Photo courtesy of the San Jacinto Museum of History Association

A century later the tale had been turned into song. The girl was called the Yellow Rose in reference to her skin color: She is supposed to have been a light-skinned black woman, "high yellow" in the vernacular of the times.

There are those, however, who believe she was a real person.

According to historian Stephen Harrigan, her name was Emily Morgan and she was an "indentured servant" who became part of the goods confiscated by Santa Anna as his army swept across Texas. Ever loyal to Texas, she did what she could to distract the general, and the rest is . . . legend.

In other accounts she is a free black woman named Emily West who signed a contract with James Morgan in New York City on October 25, 1835, to work for one year as housekeeper at the New Washington Association's hotel in Morgan's Point, Texas. She was to receive $100 for the year and transportation to Galveston Bay. But she was seized by Mexican troops on April 16, 1836, in a roundup of black and white denizens of New Washington.

As the climactic battle of the Texas Revolution approached, she either: a) was an unwilling partner for Santa Anna, b) saw an opportunity to help the Texans and did what was in her power to distract the general, c) seduced Santa Anna after sending another servant to warn Sam Houston, or d) none of the above.

Many historians correctly point out that Emily, if she existed, would have had no way of knowing Sam Houston's plans or even how close his troops were to the Mexican army.

There are documents in the Texas State Archives showing that a thirty-six-year-old free black woman named Emily D. West applied for and received a passport to return to New York City in 1837. A note from a man named Isaac Moreland says she had lost the papers showing she was a freeperson at the San Jacinto battleground.

Regardless of which account (if any) you believe, the fact remains: The person may or may not have existed, but the legend is here to stay.

· Ladies of the Links ·

Texas has bragging rights for two of the greatest woman golfers of the 1900s: **Babe Didrikson Zaharias** and **Betsy Rawls.**

Babe Didrikson Zaharias Sites

Standing head and putter above all the places devoted to Babe is the **Babe Didrikson Zaharias Museum and Visitor Center** in Beaumont. A gleaming little domed structure, it boasts eighteen glass-fronted cases displaying her trophies, Olympic medals, golf clubs, and more personal items such as a tea service and a boomerang she brought back from her honeymoon in Australia, plus many, many, many photos.

Hours: 9 A.M. to 5 P.M. daily. Closed Christmas
Admission: Free
Location: Alongside Interstate 10 in Beaumont. Take exit
    854 off I-10. If you're heading east, loop under the
    freeway. The museum is on its north side.
Phone Number: 409-833-4622
Address: 1750 E. Interstate 10, Beaumont, TX 77704
Web Address: www.babedidricksonzaharias.org

The Museum of the Gulf Coast in Port Arthur has a display on Babe, including golf clubs, a trophy, and photographs.

Hours: 9 A.M. to 5 P.M., Mon.-Sat., 1 to 5 P.M. Sundays
Admission: $3.50 adults, $3 senior citizens, $1.50 children
    6 to 18, 50 cents children younger than 6

The Babe Didrikson Zaharias Museum in Beaumont

Location: Second floor of the museum in its Sports Hall.
　　To get to the museum, take Highway 69 south from
　　Beaumont. Drive all the way through town to Procter
　　Street. Take a right and drive past Lamar State Col-
　　lege. Turn left on Beaumont Avenue then take the
　　first left into the museum parking lot. It is across the
　　street from the City of Port Arthur Police
　　Department.
Phone Number: 409-982-7000
Address: 700 Procter, Port Arthur, TX 77640
Web Address: www.pa.lamar.edu/museum/gulf.html

Babe is buried in **Forest Lawn Memorial Park** in Beaumont,
4955 Pine Street. To get there take the Pine Street exit off I-10
and go north. It winds around quite a bit, and you'll pass several
other cemeteries. As you near Forest Lawn you'll see low
stone walls. They flank the cemetery's entrance. (If you see the
Beaumont Country Club, you've gone too far on Pine Street.)
Just inside the cemetery entrance you'll see a yellow building
with green shutters on the left. Turn right, away from the building, at the first road. Then turn at the first left that you come to.
The graveside will be on the left, in a triangular plot well
shaded by trees. There is a historical marker on the left.

The Life of Babe Didrikson Zaharias

The girl who would conquer the worlds of basketball, track, and
golf was born June 26, 1911, in Port Arthur, Texas, to Norwe-
gian immigrants Hannah and Ole. The family moved to
Beaumont in 1915.

　　Her real name was Mildred Ella, but she was soon dubbed
"Babe" by pals who thought she swung a bat like Babe Ruth. An
indifferent student at Beaumont High School, Babe excelled at
sports.

　　During her senior year of high school she was recruited by
Employers Casualty Company of Dallas to play on its semi-

professional women's basketball team, the Golden Cyclones. From 1930 to 1932 she led the team to two finals and a national championship and was voted All-American each season.

In 1932 she expanded her repertoire and represented the company as a one-woman team at the 1932 Amateur Athletic Union Championships. She placed first in five events: shot put, javelin and baseball throws, eighty-meter hurdles, and long jump and tied for first in the high jump. She placed fourth in the discus throw. Babe broke four world records and single-handedly racked up more points than the entire second-place team.

Thanks to that performance she qualified for the 1932 Olympics in the javelin throw, hurdles, and high jump. She won gold medals in the javelin throw and hurdles, and a silver in the high jump. Plus, she broke world records in all three events.

Babe turned pro after returning home to capitalize on her fame and earn money to help her family. Among other things, she toured with several basketball teams, pitched in minor league spring training games, and participated in a billiards tour.

During this time, when she was between gigs, Babe was learning golf. In April of 1933 she won her first title, the Texas Women's Amateur Championship—the second golf tournament she ever entered. She was subsequently barred from competing as an amateur, so she went back on the tour circuit.

In 1938 she qualified for the Los Angeles Open, a men's Professional Golfers' Association tournament, and while there she met George Zaharias, a famous professional wrestler and sports promoter. They married that December.

Babe was reinstated as an amateur golfer in 1943 and subsequently won seventeen consecutive tournaments, becoming, in the process, the first American woman to win the British Women's Amateur Championship. She turned pro in 1947 and continued her winning ways. In 1948 she became a charter member of the Ladies Professional Golf Association and went on to become its top money winner from 1949 to 1951.

Babe in the 1930s
Photo courtesy of Lamar University/
Babe Didrikson Zaharias Foundation

In 1950 the Associated Press voted her Woman Athlete of the Half-Century.

She had professional success, but something was missing from her home life—a child. She and her husband tried to adopt, but strict rules kept them from qualifying.

In 1953 she was diagnosed with colon cancer and had a colostomy that April. Fourteen weeks later she was back on the links, and the Golf Writers of America gave her the Ben Hogan Trophy as comeback player of the year.

The following year she won five tournaments. But the cancer recurred in 1955, and Babe was finally forced to stop playing. She died at John Sealy Hospital in Galveston on September 27, 1956. She was forty-five.

Betsy Rawls Site

Betsy's exploits are chronicled—along with those of other gal golfers, including Babe Didrikson Zaharias—at the **Texas Golf Hall of Fame**.

Hours: Vary

Admission: Free

Location: Directly behind the 18th green of the Tournaments Players Course in Spring, Texas (a Houston suburb). To get there, take Interstate 45 north from Houston. Take exit 73 towards Rayford Road/Sawdust Road. Turn left onto Rayford Road. It turns into Sawdust Road then into Grogan's Mill Road. Turn right onto S. Millbend Drive and you'll see the golf course.

Phone Number: 281-364-7270

Address: 1730 S. Millbend Dr., Spring, TX 77380

Web Address: www.ldrs.com/fame/

The Life of Betsy Rawls

South Carolina native Betsy Rawls never picked up a golf club until she was in her late teens, but she was good enough to make the team at the University of Texas when she started classes there. In 1949, a mere four years after trying the game for the first time, Betsy won the Women's Texas Golf Association title and the Women's Trans-National. The following year she won the state title again, along with the Broadmoor Invitational.

Betsy turned pro as soon as she graduated from college in 1951. Her first year on the Ladies Professional Golf Association tour she won three titles, including the U.S. Women's Open. She won at least two tournaments every year from 1951 to 1962, including ten in 1959. From 1963 to 1966 she won at least one tournament a year.

She led the tour in victories in 1952, 1957, and 1959. In total, she captured fifty-five LPGA titles during her career.

Easy-going and cheerful, she was popular with other golfers.

Betsy retired from playing in 1975, then served six years as the LPGA's Tournament Director. She later became the first woman to serve on the Rules Committee for the men's U.S. Open.

· A Reformer in Bloom ·

Claudia Alta "Lady Bird" Taylor Johnson Sites

She gained fame as the wife of a senator-turned-president from Texas, but Claudia Taylor "Lady Bird" Johnson carved out her own piece of Texas history and created her own colorful legacy.

Without question, the best "sight" related to Lady Bird Johnson is the annual profusion of wildflowers along Texas highways in the spring, the result of years of dedication to state beautification and preservation, which led to the Highway Beautification Act of 1965.

She also founded **The Lady Bird Johnson Wildflower Center**, a nonprofit organization dedicated to educating people "about the environmental necessity, economic value, and natural beauty of native plants." The center has a visitors gallery, extensive gardens, a store, and a café.

Hours: The grounds are open 9 A.M. to 5:30 P.M. Tues.-Sun, visitors gallery open 9 A.M. to 4 P.M. Saturdays and 1 to 4 P.M. Sundays. No pets allowed. Call to schedule group tours.

Admission: $7 adults, $5.50 students and senior citizens, free to children younger than 4 and wildflower center members. Tour discount available.

Location: Southwest Austin. From Interstate 35, take exit 226B toward Slaughter Lane. Turn onto Slaughter Lane going west. Proceed about six miles and turn left onto South Mo Pac Expressway. In about a mile, turn left onto La Crosse Avenue. The facility is on the right.

Claudia Alta Taylor, age three
Photo courtesy LBJ Library and Museum

Phone Number: 512-292-4200
Address: 4801 La Crosse Avenue, Austin, TX 78739
Web Address: www.wildflower.org

The visitors center at the park headquarters for the **Lyndon B. Johnson National Historical Park** offers a display and a thirty-minute video about the former first lady. The visitors center is in one section of the LBJ National Historical Park. The **LBJ Ranch** (and Lady Bird's current residence) is in the other section of the park, fourteen miles from park headquarters. (See the next entry for information about the ranch.)

> *Hours*: The visitors center is open 8:45 A.M. to 5 P.M. daily. Closed Thanksgiving, Christmas Day, and New Year's Day.
> *Admission*: Free
> *Location*: In Johnson City, 50 miles west of Austin along Highway 290 and 60 miles north of San Antonio on Highway 290. The park is well marked and hard to miss.
> *Phone Number*: 830-868-7128
> *Address*: P.O. Box 329, Johnson City, TX 79636
> *Web Address*: www.nps.gov/lyjo/home.htm

Lady Bird still lives in the ranch house on one part of the Lyndon B. Johnson National Historical Park. Public tours of the ranch are available. During LBJ's presidency the house was called the Texas White House. All tours leave from the LBJ State Historical Park.

> *Hours*: Bus tours depart 10 A.M. to 4 P.M.
> *Admission*: $3 for anyone older than six, under six free
> *Location*: From the visitors center at the national park headquarters, take Highway 290 fourteen miles west to the LBJ State Historical Park. Tickets for the LBJ

Ranch bus tours are purchased at the State Park Visitors Center.

Phone Number: 830-868-7128
Address: P.O. Box 329, Johnson City, TX 79636
Web Address: www.nps.gov/lyjo/home.htm

The **First Lady's Gallery** at the **Lyndon Baines Johnson Library and Museum** in Austin explores Lady's Bird's legacy as a humanitarian, an unofficial diplomat, and a champion of nature with photographs, letters, and memorabilia.

Hours: 9 A.M. to 5 P.M. daily. Closed Christmas Day
Admission: Free
Location: In Austin. From Interstate 35, take the 26th Street exit and proceed west to Red River Street. Turn left. The library is about a quarter mile on the left.
Phone Number: 512-916-5137
Address: 2313 Red River Street, Austin, Texas 78705
Web Address: www.lbjlib.utexas.edu/

Lady Bird was born in a pretty house just outside of **Karnack**, Texas. The two-story structure, built before the Civil War, is constructed of white bricks made by slaves. It is not open to the public, but it is visible from the road. From Marshall, take Highway 43 north. The house is perched on a hill on the right side of the road about twelve miles from Marshall. It is about three miles south of Karnack.

The Life of Lady Bird Johnson

Born in Karnack on December 22, 1912, she was christened Claudia Alta Taylor. But she wasn't called "Claudia" by the family for long. Her nursemaid remarked that Claudia was "as purty as a lady bird," and from then on she was known as Lady

Bird. Her mother died when she was five years old, leaving her in the care of her father, Thomas, and older brothers Tommy and Tony. An aunt, Effie Pattillo, soon moved to Karnack to care for the children.

Lady Bird graduated from Marshall High School in Marshall, Texas, in 1928 then attended Saint Mary's Episcopal School for Girls in Dallas from 1928 to 1930. She began classes at the University of Texas in 1930, and in 1933 got a bachelor's degree in history. She stayed in school and earned a journalism degree in 1934.

That same year, she met Lyndon Baines Johnson, who was visiting Austin on official business as a congressional secretary. When he asked for a date within minutes of meeting her, she accepted. What followed was truly a passionate, whirlwind courtship. Johnson had to return to Washington, but he bombarded her with love letters, telegrams, and telephone calls. When he returned to Texas seven weeks after their initial meeting, he proposed and she accepted. She later said: "Sometimes Lyndon simply takes your breath away." They married on November 17, 1934, at Saint Mark's Episcopal Church in San Antonio.

She wanted a family but suffered several miscarriages before giving birth to Lynda Bird in 1944. Lynda Bird's sister, Luci, was born in 1947.

Lady Bird assisted her husband throughout his political career, even helping keep his congressional office open during World War II when he volunteered for naval service. After a heart attack sidelined him in 1955 when he was senate majority leader, she stepped in to help run his office until he could return to work.

Johnson once said his constituents "would happily have elected her over me."

When Johnson became vice president in 1961, she saw an opportunity to put her unasked-for fame and influence to good use, and she seized it by becoming a goodwill ambassador.

Lady Bird Johnson at the White House
Photo courtesy LBJ Library and Museum

She was unexpectedly thrust into the role of first lady when John F. Kennedy was assassinated in 1963. In her new role she was a strong supporter of the Head Start program and other anti-poverty initiatives, and she created the First Lady's Committee for a More Beautiful Capital, which led to a nationwide beautification effort and the 1965 Highway Beautification Act.

In 1970, after her husband had left office, she published an account of her years as first lady called *A White House Diary*. She said at the time, "I was keenly aware that I had a unique opportunity, a front row seat, on an unfolding story and nobody else was going to see it from quite the vantage point that I saw it."

She returned to Texas and the family ranch in Stonewall after her stint as first lady. The same year, the Johnsons donated the ranch to the national park service with the caveat that they could live out their lives there.

Lady Bird was widowed in 1973.

Over the next several decades she continued her volunteer work, most notably in support of environmental preservation. In 1982 she provided the idea, the land, and the money to start the nonprofit National Wildflower Center. It opened in honor of her seventieth birthday and was later renamed in her honor.

She received scores of awards for her works, most notably the Medal of Freedom in 1977 and the Congressional Gold Medal in 1988. Today, Lady Bird continues her support for organizations such as the National Geographic Society, the University of Texas, and of course, the wildflower center she started. She splits her time between the ranch and a home in Austin.

· From Texas to Temperance ·

Carry Nation Site

Long before she became the hatchet-wielding mama of the prohibitionist movement, Carry Nation lived in Texas.

There is a **historical marker** at the site of The Old Columbia Hotel, which was operated by Carry in East Columbia around 1880. To get there, leave West Columbia heading east on Texas 35. Watch closely for a road sign eight-tenths of a mile after leaving West Columbia and bear right on the road it indicates to East Columbia. In East Columbia, continue until you reach Front Street. Turn left. The marker will be on your left.

The Life of Carry Nation

Carry Nation made her reputation railing against the evils of tobacco and alcohol. But she began life much more quietly on November 25, 1846, when she was born in Kentucky. Her mother suffered from mental illness, so Carry—a sickly child—was often left in the hands of the family slaves. Her father was restless and frequently moved the family in his quest for a better situation.

On November 21, 1867, Carry married Dr. Charles Gloyd—a move that would shape her life in radical ways. Gloyd was an alcoholic, and Carry left him around the time their only child, a daughter named Charlien, was born. He died soon afterward.

Carry got a teaching certificate and taught for four years before marrying David Nation in 1877. Together, they moved to Texas in 1879 and tried cotton farming on 1,700 acres near Houston. But the farming and the marriage were troubled ventures. Carry took a job managing a hotel in East Columbia while they tried to sell their farm, and her husband moved to Brazoria to practice law. Carry's daughter, step-daughter, and mother-in-law lived with her, and it was up to Carry to support them all. Eventually the family reconciled, sold their land, and bought a hotel in Richmond, Texas.

It was while in Richmond that Carry came to believe God had chosen her for a special mission. She was barred by the Methodist and Episcopal churches from teaching in their Sunday schools, so she started her own weekly class at the hotel.

The family moved to Medicine Lodge, Kansas, in 1889, and David became a pastor in the Christian Church. Carry denounced his preaching for its lack of fire. Her own increasingly radical views got her expelled from the Christian Church. During this time she became known in Kansas for her charitable works, especially among those affected by alcoholism. She never forgot the effect alcohol had on her first husband.

In 1892 she became co-founder of a local chapter of the Woman's Christian Temperance Union, but she was never fully embraced by the WCTU thanks to the extreme nature of her words and actions. She began wreaking destruction on establishments that produced and sold liquor, and in 1900 she took up the hatchet for the first time.

Her husband divorced her the following year.

Carry was arrested more than thirty times for her prohibitionist activities, but she was undeterred. She toured the nation giving lectures to support herself. When she spoke on college campuses, students delighted in duping her into believing that members of the faculty were drunks.

Carry became increasingly frail in her later years, and her public appearances became less frequent. After collapsing in Arkansas during a speech in January of 1911, she spent the last months of her life in a Kansas hospital where she died on June 2, 1911.

· West Texas Woman ·

Annie Riggs Site

Which came first, the fame or the museum? It's hard to say whether Annie was so well-known that a museum was started in her honor, or whether she became famous because of the museum.

The **Annie Riggs Memorial Museum** occupies a rambling structure in Fort Stockton that was once a hotel owned by Annie. It includes pictures of Annie and memorabilia from her life, as well as a grab bag of artifacts relating to the history of the town. Some of the rooms are preserved as they were when Annie owned the hotel.

Hours: September through May—10 A.M. to noon
Mon.-Sat., 1:30 to 5:30 P.M. Sundays; June through
August—10 A.M. to 8 P.M. Mon.-Sat., 1:30 to 8 P.M.
Sundays

Admission: $2 adults, $1.50 senior citizens, $1 children
age 6-12, free for children under 6

Location: In Fort Stockton. From Interstate 10, exit at
FM 1053 and go south. FM 1053 is also called Main
Street. The museum is on the left, at the intersection
of Main and Callaghan Streets.

Phone Number: 915-336-2167

Address: 301 S. Main Street, Fort Stockton, TX 79735

Web Address: None

Annie Riggs
Photo courtesy of Fort Stockton Historical Society

The Life of Annie Riggs

Annie's reputation wasn't far reaching, but folks in Pecos County certainly knew who she was.

Born November 24, 1858, in New Mexico, she moved with her family to Fort Stockton, Texas, when she was eight years old. Annie was married twice, not an unusual occurrence for those times. But she was divorced twice, too. And that was outside the norms of the day. She first married James Johnson, a sheriff, in 1877. They had six children together, and during their marriage she ran a boarding house. They divorced in the 1880s. In September of 1891 Annie married Barney Kemp Riggs, a man who had been convicted (but later pardoned) of murder. Many people considered him a hired gun.

She had four children with Riggs but divorced him in 1901.

Eventually, she bought the hotel that bears her name with the proceeds from her second husband's estate. Riggs was shot during a quarrel with Annie's son-in-law in 1902, a year after his divorce from Annie.

Annie reportedly took Riggs to the Koehler Hotel after he was shot and stayed with him until he died the following afternoon. He didn't have a will, so a court eventually awarded his estate to Annie. She used the proceeds to buy the Koehler Hotel in 1904 and operated it for most of the rest of her life. It was a rare thing at that time in that place for a woman to own and operate a business.

Annie died on May 17, 1931. She was seventy-three.

· Sanctified and Vilified ·

Martha White McWhirter Sites

Martha White McWhirter was a deeply religious woman whose convictions led her to start the Belton Woman's Commonwealth, more commonly known as the Sanctificationists. To the delight of the women who joined, it empowered them to take charge of their own lives. But to the dismay of those women's husbands, the movement also demanded celibacy. The Sanctificationists are long gone, but Belton still has a few reminders of them.

The **Bell County Museum** maintains an extensive timeline display on its second floor, and the staff there is always happy to answer questions.

Hours: 1 to 5 P.M. Tues.-Sat. Group tours and other hours
   by appointment
Admission: Free
Location: 201 North Main Street in downtown Belton,
   about two blocks from the courthouse square. Take
   I-35 to Belton, just south of Temple, and take exit
   294A. Turn right (if you're driving from the north—
   left if from the south) onto E. Central Avenue. Drive
   past the courthouse square. Turn right onto Main
   Street. The museum is one-tenth of a mile on the
   right. Parking is in the back.
Phone Number: 254-933-5243
Mailing Address: P.O. Box 1381, Belton, Texas 76513
Web Address: www.vvm.com/~museum/

Martha McWhirter's home in Belton

The house where Martha lived, first with her husband, then with her sister Sanctificationists, is just a few blocks from the museum at 400 N. Pearl Street. From the museum's front door, turn right on Main Street and walk to the light at the corner of E. 2nd Avenue. Cross Main Street at the light and walk one block to N. Pearl Street. Cross E. 2nd Avenue on N. Pearl and proceed about a half block to the house, which will be on the left-hand side of the street. It's pale stone with green shutters and a historical marker affixed to its front.

The Life of Martha McWhirter and the Sanctificationists

Martha White was born on May 17, 1827, in Gainesboro, Tennessee, to a gentleman farmer and his wife. Little is known of her early life. She married George M. McWhirter in 1845 and bore him twelve children.

The family moved to Bell County, Texas, ten years later. It would be ten more years before they moved into the growing

Martha McWhirter
Photo courtesy of the Lena Armstrong Public Library in Belton

little town of Belton. They were devout people and co-founded an interdenominational Sunday school in town. Martha also led a weekly woman's prayer group and was a regular churchgoer.

Her life changed dramatically in 1866. Distraught over the recent deaths of two of her children, Martha came to believe that God was punishing her. One day while walking home from church she had a vision: The ritualism of the church was wrong, and she was supposed to do something about it. Believing that she had been "sanctified" by this vision, she became an implacable opponent of traditional organized religion. Martha shared her experience and her conviction with her prayer group. As Martha had done, they began praying about the problems they faced at home. Often these "problems" came in the form of alcoholic or abusive husbands. Very soon a number of these women became "sanctified" too. A movement was born.

Under Martha's leadership, they began taking odd jobs—hauling wood, nursing, taking in laundry, cleaning homes—in order to earn money to become financially independent. The work was hard for some of the women, who were serving in houses where they had once been welcomed as guests. But few left the group.

All the money went into a common fund for the greater good of the group. Many of the women left abusive home situations, and Martha took them in. At first the movement did not cause much of a stir in the community. The women were providing valuable services to their neighbors and were quiet in the practice of their new beliefs. Plus, Martha was a powerful woman in the community and could get away with things that a less prominent person might not.

Eventually the women began following yet another of Martha's divine dictates: Those who continued to live in their own homes had as little as possible to do with their "unsanctified" husbands. The sanctified, she said, were to separate themselves from those who were not.

Predictably, the menfolk were unhappy with this development. Some even became violent, prompting more women to flee to Martha's house. The scorned husbands and some of the townspeople began to blame the group in general—and Martha in particular—for a growing number of divorces in the town. Martha was even named in a few of the divorces. The Sanctificationists often got the last laugh, however. When a husband died before his wife, she and the Sanctificationists inherited his property.

Finally, there were so many Sanctificationists that they crowded George out of his house. He and Martha separated, and he moved into rooms above the store he owned in town— rooms Martha fixed up for him. If it had been up to him, they would have stayed together, but Martha was adamant in her beliefs. She was sanctified. He was not. So George moved out but continued supporting her, financially as well as emotionally, and he defended her in public whenever the situation demanded it.

When there were too many Sanctificationists for Martha's house, members began moving into other properties owned by members. The women converted one of their properties into a boarding house and another into a commercial laundry to increase the group's income. In 1886 the group bought a hotel and added its revenues to the group's coffers. George died in 1887 and left his property to Martha. At its height, the group had about thirty members at any one time. The people of Belton eventually became reconciled to the group, even welcomed it in some cases. Martha was the first woman elected to the city Board of Trade, and her name was included on the cornerstone of the Belton opera house.

The Sanctificationists weren't single-minded. They believed in education and travel and got as much of both as they could. Eventually their book collection was so large and so popular with the people of Belton, it was used to start the town's first public library.

Around the turn of the century the women decided to leave Belton. They sold their extensive land holdings and bought property near Washington, D.C.

Martha died there on April 21, 1904.

· Indian Captives ·

Cynthia Ann Parker, Rachel Parker Plummer, and Elizabeth Kellogg Site

Cynthia Ann Parker and her cousin, Rachel Parker Plummer, were among five people captured when Fort Parker was attacked by a large band of Kiowa, Kichai, and Comanche warriors on May 19, 1836. Both were eventually returned to their Anglo families after spending many years with the Indians, though Cynthia returned unwillingly. Another relative, Elizabeth Kellogg, was also captured during the attack but was ransomed for $150 soon afterward by Sam Houston. Fort Parker has been rebuilt and is now a historical park.

Old Fort Parker Historical Park sits in a clearing outside of Groesbeck, about forty miles east of Waco. The stockade was rebuilt, as far as possible, on the exact site of the original fort in 1936 and again in 1967. Cabins along the interior fort walls hold a variety of displays about the fort, its occupants, Texas frontier life during the earliest days of the Republic of Texas, and the attack that devastated the original Fort Parker.

Hours: 9 A.M. to 5 P.M. daily

Admission: $2 adults, $1 children 6 to 11, free for children under 6

Location: Take Highway 14 out of Groesbeck four miles north to Park Road 35. Turn left and follow the park road to the fort.

Phone Number: 254-729-5253

Address: RR 3 Box 746, Groesbeck, TX 76642

Web Address: www.tpwd.state.tx.us/park/oldfort/

The Life of Rachel Parker Plummer

Rachel Parker was born in Illinois on March 22, 1819, to Martha and James Parker. By 1830 three of her siblings had died from disease, so Rachel's father decided to move the family. After a brief stay in Arkansas, they settled in Texas in 1833.

On May 28, 1833, Rachel married a farmer named Luther Thomas Martin Plummer, and on January 6, 1835, she had their first son, James Pratt. Not long after his birth, the three joined about thirty other people who moved to Fort Parker. Also in the group were Rachel's aunt, Elizabeth Kellogg, and her cousin, Cynthia Ann Parker.

On May 19, 1836, Rachel's husband was working on a farm about a mile away from the fort when a band of Comanches, Kiowas, and Kichai warriors attacked the fort, killing five men including Rachel's grandfather. The pregnant Rachel tried to escape with her year-old son, but as she reported later, "A large sulky looking Indian picked up a hoe and knocked me down."

The captives were soon divided up, and Rachel was sold as a slave to another Comanche tribe. Her son James went with a different tribe, and she never saw him again. In October she gave birth to her second son and named him Luther. When the child was about six weeks old Rachel watched as the child was strangled then dragged to his death.

In all, she spent about a year and a half with the Comanche before being ransomed by Mexican traders. They, in turn, took her to an American couple, Col. and Mrs. William Donoho, living in Santa Fe, who had arranged for her ransom. Rachel was very thin and ill, and her body was crisscrossed with scars.

Within weeks political turmoil caused the Donohos to flee to Missouri, taking Rachel with them. She waited there until a family member could fetch her and take her back to Texas, where she was reunited with her husband on February 19, 1838. After her rescue she published an account of her experiences.

Rachel gave birth to her third child on January 4, 1839. She was very ill and died on March 19, 1839, in Houston. Her baby died two days later.

The Life of Cynthia Ann Parker

Cynthia Ann Parker was born sometime between June 2, 1824, and May 31, 1825, to Lucy and Silas Parker in Illinois. The family moved to Fort Parker in about 1835. She was there on the morning of May 19, 1836, when a large band of Comanche, Kiowa, and Kichai warriors arrived in the clearing outside the fort. Cynthia, who was about nine years old at the time, watched along with the other settlers as her uncle Benjamin Parker was killed when he tried to negotiate with the Indians.

Then the band attacked. Cynthia's father was killed, and she fled with her mother, six-year-old brother John, and two younger children. They were soon surrounded by Indians and split up. Cynthia and John were put on horses with warriors, and the rest were taken back to the fort where they were soon rescued.

Cynthia and John, along with their cousin Rachel Plummer and her son James, and Rachel's aunt, Elizabeth Kellogg, had all been captured. The war party traveled north. All the captives, even Rachel's year-old son, were beaten. On about the sixth day, the captives were split up.

Little is known of Cynthia's life with the Comanche after that. She rarely spoke of it after she was recaptured. Cynthia assimilated with the Comanche, married Chief Peta Nocona, and had three children with him: Quanah, Pecos, and Topsannah.

Her white family never stopped looking for her, though. There are a number of unconfirmed reports that she had several chances to be ransomed but declined, preferring instead to stay with her Comanche family. Her brother John was ransomed in 1846 and, according to one of the stories, visited with her twice in an attempt to coax her back to her birth family. She

Cynthia Ann Parker and daughter Topsannah shortly
after their "liberation" from the Commanche.
Photo courtesy of The Texas Collection at Baylor University

reportedly told him that she loved her Indian family and friends and could not leave them.

On December 18, 1860, Texas Rangers attacked a Comanche band near the Pease River. Cynthia was among the Indians and fled on horseback with her infant daughter, but was captured.

The attackers were surprised to discover the woman they captured had blue eyes. Though she spoke no English and appeared in every other way to be Comanche, they determined she was a captive and set out to find her family.

Cynthia's uncle, Isaac Parker, questioned the thirty-four-year-old woman, but at first she said nothing. When he turned to a companion and said, "If this is my niece, her name is Cynthia Ann," she supposedly recognized her name, leaped up, and exclaimed, "Me Cynthia Ann." Under further questioning with a translator, she recalled having white parents at one time and was able to give some details of the raid on Fort Parker.

Cynthia Ann wished to be reunited with her Comanche family, but the Parkers would not hear of it. She and her daughter went to live with an uncle north of Fort Worth, and the family tried to reassimilate her. Cynthia resisted and tried to escape. Rumors circulated that the family locked her up to keep her from running away.

On April 8, 1861, the Texas Legislature voted her a pension of $100 per year for five years to compensate her for her captivity.

Later that same year she went to live with her brother Isaac and his wife in Van Zandt County. She participated in the life of the household but still longed to return to the Comanche. The Parkers allegedly promised she could visit the Comanche, but the visit never happened.

Eventually Cynthia Ann and Topsannah went to live with her sister. Topsannah learned English quickly and was assimilating to her new life. But in 1863 she contracted a fever and died on December 15. She was five years old.

Cynthia Ann was grief-stricken. According to some accounts, she starved herself to death the following year. However, according to census records, she was still living in 1870. It is likely she died in 1870.

Cynthia Ann was buried near her final home but was eventually moved to a cemetery in Oklahoma at the behest of her son, Quanah, who had become a chief of the Comanche.

· Doyenne of a Ranching Dynasty ·

Henrietta King Sites

Richard King started the now famous **King Ranch** in 1853, but it grew and prospered under the leadership of his widow, Henrietta.

> *Hours*: Visitor Center—9 A.M. to 4 P.M., Mon.-Sat., noon to 5 P.M. Sundays; Ranch tours vary by season. Call for times or check the Web site.
>
> *Admission*: Varies depending on the tour. Several are offered. Call or check the Web site.
>
> *Location*: Just west of Kingsville off Highway 141
>
> *Phone Number*: 361-592-8055
>
> *Address*: Highway 141 West, P.O. Box 1090, Kingsville, TX 78364-1090
>
> *Web Address*: www.king-ranch.com

Henrietta is buried in section B lot 1 at **Chamberlain Cemetery,** 735 East Caesar Avenue in Kingsville. 512-592-1371.

The Life of Henrietta King

Henrietta, the only child of Maria and Hiram Chamberlain, was born July 21, 1832, in Boonville, Missouri. Her mother died in 1835 and her father was away from home a lot with his work as a Presbyterian missionary, so she was often left to her own devices as a child.

When she was fourteen years old, she was sent to the Female Institute in Holly Springs, Mississippi. She stayed

Henrietta Maria Morse Chamberlain King, in mourning dress. The brooch at her throat is a picture of Capt. Richard King, her late husband.
Photo courtesy of The UT Institute of Texan Cultures at San Antonio

there for about two years. By early 1850 Henrietta was living with her father in Brownsville, Texas.

After a brief stint teaching at the Rio Grande Female Institute, Henrietta married rancher Richard King on December 10,

1854, and they moved to a little house made of mud and sticks on 75,000 acres King had purchased the previous year.

During the Civil War, while pregnant with the last of her five children, Henrietta was at the ranch (but her husband was not) when Union cavalry raided the place and ransacked the house. Afterward she moved the children to San Antonio, but the family returned to the ranch in 1866.

Henrietta King is described in family papers as mild-mannered but with an iron will. She managed housing for the Mexican ranch hands and established informal classes for their children.

She was widowed in 1885 and inherited her husband's 500,000 acres of land and $500,000 in debt. Together with her son-in-law she worked to eradicate the debt and expand the ranch. By 1895 it had expanded to 650,000 acres and was experimenting with a variety of new livestock breeds and new methods of farming. That year Henrietta gave her son-in-law her power of attorney. While she retained a keen interest in the ranch, she turned her attention to other pursuits.

Shortly after the turn of the century she gave 75,000 acres of right-of-way for a railroad. In 1904 she donated land for two towns along that railroad. One of them was named Kingsville in honor of the King family. Henrietta either started or invested in at least seven businesses in the new town—everything from lumber to power and publishing. She also donated land for four churches in the new town—Baptist, Methodist, Episcopal, and Catholic—and paid to build a Presbyterian church. Henrietta financed a public high school for the town and gave land for the Texas-Mexican Industrial Institute, South Texas State Teachers College (now Texas A&M University—Kingsville), and the Spohn Hospital. Kingsville truly was the Town That Henrietta Built.

When Henrietta died on March 31, 1925, at the age of ninety-two, the King Ranch had grown to 1.2 million acres and was home to 94,000 head of cattle.

· The Mother of Texas ·

Jane Long Sites

Most of Jane Long's remarkable story was related to Mirabeau B. Lamar when he was writing a history of Texas. She has not achieved the same fame as the "fathers" of Texas. But there are a few legends and few places to visit.

She operated a boardinghouse in Richmond, and there is a **historical marker** there at the spot where it once stood. In Richmond, a little town just southwest of Houston, take Highway ALT 90 through town. (It's also called Jackson Street.) Turn north on N. Fourth Street. Where it intersects with Morton Street, look for Fort Bend Postal Service. Park there and walk around two buildings to the back of the store. The marker is there.

Jane is buried in **Morton Cemetery** in Richmond. From ALT 90, turn north onto 2ⁿᵈ Street (it's near the Brazos River crossing). Go straight, over the train tracks, and proceed about half a mile. The cemetery is on the left at Commerce Street. It closes at dark.

The Life of Jane Wilkinson Long

Jane Wilkinson was born on July 23, 1798, in Charles County, Maryland, the tenth child of William and Anne Wilkinson. Her father died less than two years after she was born. About ten years after that Jane's mother moved the family to Mississippi Territory, where she died about two years later, in 1813. Jane went to live with her older sister, Barbara, on a plantation near Natchez, and it is there that she met her fate in the form of

James Long, a soldier returning from the Battle of New Orleans. They married on May 14, 1815.

After four years in Mississippi, Long set off for Texas, leaving a very pregnant Jane and their three-year-old daughter Ann in the care of one of Jane's sisters. Their second child, Rebecca, was born June 16. In 1819 Jane left both girls in the care of a maid and a sister living in Louisiana then set off to join her husband. But she could not find him, and within months of her arrival in Nacogdoches, she had to flee with other Americans when Spanish soldiers threatened the town.

James Long was returning to the area from a trip to Galveston and met up with Jane during that time. Jane returned to her sister's home to find that her daughter, Rebecca, had died. Leaving her surviving daughter with a different sister, Jane returned to Texas. The Longs went to Bolivar, on the coast, and ever after Jane claimed to have had dinner with the pirate Jean Lafitte.

By 1821 all three of the Longs were living on the Bolivar Peninsula. On September 19, 1821, Jane's husband left on a month-long business trip and never returned. He was captured by Spanish soldiers and died in Mexico City on April 8, 1822.

But Jane knew none of this. She knew only that he had promised to return, and she was determined to wait for him— even when the other families left Bolivar, leaving the pregnant-again Jane alone with her maid, Kian, and daughter Ann.

She gave birth to her third daughter, Mary James, on December 21, 1821, in an ice-covered tent. Jane claimed to be the first white woman to give birth in Texas—a myth that took hold and earned for her the nickname "Mother of Texas." In fact, many Anglos had given birth in Texas before Jane.

In the early spring of 1822, Jane finally abandoned Bolivar. Her supplies were exhausted, and as she later related, the little group was constantly faced with the threat of attack from Native Americans. To prevent an attack, Jane said she and the maid designed a ruse to fool the Indians into thinking there were more people at the Bolivar fort than just Jane, the maid, and the two children.

It was midsummer before she found out that she was a widow. The following year she returned to her sister's home in Louisiana, where Mary James died in 1824. Soon thereafter the entire family—Jane, her surviving daughter Ann, and her sister's family—returned to Texas where Jane received land in Fort Bend and Waller Counties from Stephen F. Austin.

Legend has it that many of Texas's most eligible bachelors (Ben Milam, Sam Houston, Mirabeau B. Lamar) courted her to no avail. She never remarried.

In 1837 she moved to the Fort Bend land for the first time and there she farmed and opened a boarding house. She lived there for the rest of her life and died on December 30, 1880. She was eighty-two.

· Texas Bad Girl ·

Bonnie Parker Sites

Few women have made as big a splash in Texas as Bonnie Parker, the infamous female half of Bonnie and Clyde. But two distinctly different images of Bonnie remain—callous gun moll or loyal, sensitive, bunny-loving girlfriend of a bad boy. She was a longtime resident of Dallas, and the area is full of sites with a connection to her.

The absolute best way to see Bonnie sites in North Texas is to take the Dallas Historical Society's annual **Bonnie and Clyde Tour**, usually offered in April. Participants get a bus ride complete with tour guide to sites in Dallas, Lancaster, and Irving. It's not unusual for a member of the Parker or Barrow families to show up for the tour. Cost is $25 for Dallas Historical Society members and $35 for nonmembers. The tour fills up fast, so register early. 214-421-4500.

Bonnie once spent a night in the **Kemp Calaboose** with Ralph Fults, a member of the Barrow Gang, before being transferred to a jail in Kaufman. It's a tiny little place with barred windows, behind the city hall. Kemp is an hour or so southeast of Dallas. To get there, take U.S. 175 business into town. Follow the signs to the town's business district and look for City Hall at the corner of 11th and Main Streets. The little jail is a block behind City Hall. If you can't find it, just ask. The local folks are happy to point it out.

Eagle Ford School, where Bonnie attended elementary school, is the only building on Chalk Hill Road between Singleton and West Davis Streets in Dallas. Now a private business, it's a concrete building with red and white trim. From Inter-

The Kemp Calaboose, where Bonnie Parker was once jailed overnight with Barrow gang member Ralph Fults.

state 30, take Loop 12 north. Exit at Singleton and turn right, then turn right again on Chalk Hill Road.

There is a **historical marker** in Grapevine at Dove Road and Highway 114, site of the infamous murder of two highway patrolmen by the Barrow Gang. This is where Bonnie supposedly got out of her car and "finished off" one of the victims by shooting him in the head.

Bonnie is buried at **Crown Hill Memorial Park** in Dallas. 9700 Webb Chapel Road. 214-357-3984. Her grave marker is inscribed with the improbable phrase, "As the flowers are all made sweeter by the sunshine and the dew, so this old world is made brighter by the lives of girls like you."

The Life of Bonnie Parker

Bonnie Parker was born on October 1, 1910, in Rowena, Texas, the second of Henry and Emma Parker's three children. After her father died in 1914, Bonnie's mother moved the family to Dallas, where she had family. Bonnie attended the public schools, where she excelled. She was an honor student at Eagle Ford (Elementary) School and Cement City High School.

When she was fully grown, Bonnie looked nothing like the statuesque Faye Dunaway who would one day portray her in the movies. Bonnie stood four-feet-ten and weighed less than one hundred pounds. She had blue eyes, dyed red hair, and a sparkly personality that made her a favorite with customers at the various downtown Dallas cafes where she worked. She once confided to a customer that she wanted to be a singer, actress, or poet.

Bonnie married longtime boyfriend Roy Thornton in 1926 and had "Roy and Bonnie" tattooed above her right knee to commemorate the occasion. The marriage was not a happy one, however. In late 1929 Thornton went to prison. A few months later, in January of 1930, Bonnie met Clyde Barrow.

Smitten, she began an affair with him that was interrupted the following month when he was sent to jail. In March of that year, she helped him escape by smuggling a pistol to him in his cell. He was recaptured and sent back to jail, where he stayed until 1932.

Bonnie was waiting for him when he got out, and they promptly robbed a series of grocery stores, gas stations, and small banks. Bonnie was captured after one such "job" in March 1932 and jailed overnight with one of Barrow's gang in a tiny Kemp jail before being moved to facilities in Kaufman. She was released three months later after a grand jury declined to indict her.

Afterward she reconnected with Barrow and set off on a spree that made headlines in Texas, Oklahoma, New Mexico, and Missouri. For a time they lived in Joplin, Missouri, but fled after a shootout with police that left two policemen dead. They also left behind six rolls of film that provide many of the most famous photographs of the couple, including a picture of Bonnie with a cigar in her mouth. Bonnie hated that photo and was

Bonnie Parker

Photo courtesy of The UT Institute of Texan Cultures at San Antonio,
The San Antonio Light Collection.

anxious for people to know that she did not smoke cigars. She allegedly told her mother that the cigar was a friend's, and the pose was a joke. The image so upset her that Barrow once wrote a threatening letter to Amon Carter, owner of the *Fort Worth Star-Telegram*, because the paper consistently referred to her as a cigar smoker.

In July of 1933 she was wounded along with Barrow in a shootout with police and National Guardsmen in Iowa. During the firefight Bonnie thought briefly that Barrow had been killed and she despaired. But he found her in the midst of the melee and they escaped.

Bonnie was devoted to her family and made frequent trips to Dallas—at great risk to herself. During one such visit on November 23, 1933, officers with the Dallas County Sheriff's Department almost captured her and Barrow along Highway 183 near the present-day site of Irving Mall. Bonnie was furious because her mother and Barrow's mother and sister were in a car nearby and could have been hurt during the shootout. Bonnie knew the chances she was taking—seemed, in fact, to accept her fate as inevitable. She once told her mother, "Clyde's game is up, Mama. He'll be killed sooner or later because he's never going to give up. I love him and I'm going to be with him till the end. When he dies, I want to die anyway." But as far as she was concerned, family was off limits to the lawmen.

When she couldn't visit, Bonnie sent letters. To throw off the police, she and Barrow often drove hundreds of miles from their hideouts to mail the letters. When Bonnie planned to visit in person, she or Barrow would choose a time and place, write them on a slip of paper, put the paper into an empty bottle, and have someone drive past her mother's house and toss the bottle into the yard. After making a show of being displeased with the litterbug, Bonnie's mom would retrieve the bottle. Then she'd phone Barrow's family and invite them to dinner, saying that she was making red beans that night. The dish was one of

Bonnie's favorites and was the family code that a meeting was planned.

On June 10, 1933, Bonnie was burned when Barrow's car rolled down an embankment near Wellington, Texas. They found help at a farmhouse nearby then kidnapped the people sent to investigate the accident. The investigators were released later in Oklahoma.

By 1934 Bonnie and Barrow were wanted by the authorities in a very big way. On Easter Sunday that year, in a deserted spot along Highway 114, they killed two highway patrolmen who stopped to see why Barrow and crew were parked there. According to one disputed account from a witness, Bonnie allegedly got out of the car after the officers had been shot and fired two more rounds from her sawed-off shotgun pointblank into one of their heads then exclaimed, "Look-a-there, his head bounced just like a rubber ball."

After that it was only a matter of time. They fled—first to Oklahoma, then to Louisiana. Lawmen ambushed them there in Bienville Parish on the morning of May 23, 1934. Clad in a red dress and wielding a machine gun, Bonnie died in an avalanche of gunfire aimed at Barrow's tan Ford V-8 sedan. Despite rumors to the contrary, she was not pregnant when she died. Bonnie couldn't have children. When she died, she was just twenty-three years old.

· Fly Girls ·

Many women pioneers struggled to make their way in a man's world. These gals had to make it in a man's sky. They overcame prejudice and risked considerable danger to do it, too. Airflight in its early days was a dicey thing. **Bessie Coleman** had to go all the way to France to become the first African American (man or woman) to get a pilot's license. **Katherine and Marjorie Stinson** were history-making flyers who also taught flying and established an aircraft business. Decades later the **Women Airforce Service Pilots** considered it a privilege to brave rattlesnakes and crashes, among other hazards, in order to serve their country during World War II.

These women persevered and earned their wings. Metaphors don't come any better than that.

Bessie Coleman Site

Queen Bess is one of Texas's most famous flyers, but there is surprisingly little to commemorate that fact. Her East Texas hometown of Atlanta has renamed the road to its airport in her honor, and the public library maintains a small file on her, but there is no memorial there or in Waxahachie where she also lived. Conversely, she never lived in Galveston, but the **Lone Star Flight Museum** there does have a display devoted to her. She was inducted into its Texas Aviation Hall of Fame in July 2000.

Hours: 10 A.M. to 5 P.M. daily
Admission: Free, donations encouraged

Location: Scholes International Airport at Galveston on
   Galveston Island three miles southwest of the City of
   Galveston
Phone Number: 409-740-7722
Address: 2002 Terminal Drive, Galveston, TX 77554
Web Address: www.lsfm.org

The Life of Bessie Coleman

There were no indications on January 26, 1892, that a revolutionary had just been born in the tiny town of Atlanta, Texas. The technology that would make her famous hadn't even been invented yet. But the twelfth child of George and Susan Coleman would grow up to vault gender and racial barriers. Sadly, she would never grow old.

Bessie Coleman was born into a world of poverty and racial discrimination. Seeking better opportunities, the family moved to Waxahachie within a few years of Bessie's birth. Things weren't much better there, and Bessie's father planned a move to what was then the Oklahoma Territory. But Bessie's mother refused to go and stayed with Bessie and three other daughters in Waxahachie. (Five children had already left home; four had died.)

Bessie often juggled school with backbreaking labor, picking cotton and taking in laundry to help her family survive. She went to school when she could and read as much as possible. After graduating from high school, she attended Colored Agricultural and Normal University (now Langston University) in Langston, Oklahoma, for a semester before moving to Chicago to join one of her brothers. There she attended beauty college and worked as a manicurist. In 1916 she won a contest as the best manicurist in Chicago's black community.

In 1917 Bessie married one of her brother's friends, a fellow named Claude Glenn, who was fourteen years her senior. However the two never lived together, they never publicly acknowledged the union, and Bessie never took Glenn's last name.

Bessie had long been intrigued by flying, so when her brothers returned from World War I service in France with tales of women pilots, she became determined to join their ranks. But American flying schools would not take African American students. More determined than ever, Bessie got a job managing a chili parlor (it paid better than working as a manicurist) and started saving her pennies. She took French language classes at night. By 1920 she was on her way to Le Crotoy, France, where she had found a school that would accept her as a student.

On June 15, 1921, she finished the flying course three months ahead of schedule, and the Fédération Aéronautique Internationale issued her a pilot's license. She was the first African American to become a licensed pilot, and she was among the first women to get a flying license. After a brief visit home, she returned to France for additional training in Paris. She returned to the United States determined to make a living flying and open a flying school for African Americans. (She also returned with a killer wardrobe she'd bought in Paris including a tailored flying suit.)

Bessie's first air show, at Glenn Curtiss Field on Long Island in New York on September 3, 1922, was a huge success. She barnstormed throughout the country, becoming one of the most popular stunt flyers in the United States and earning the nicknames "Queen Bess" and "Brave Bessie."

In 1924, while flying to an air show in Los Angeles, Bessie crashed after the engine in an airplane she had just bought stalled. Pilot and craft plunged 300 feet and crashed near Santa Monica. Bessie was pulled from the wreck unconscious, and it took her the better part of a year to recover from her injuries, which included a broken leg and ribs. Though she could not fly, she continued to earn money by lecturing about flying.

Fédération Aéronautique Internationale
FRANCE

Nous soussignés pouvoir sportif reconnu par la Fédération Aéronautique Internationale pour la France certifions que:

Mme *Bessie Coleman*

né à Atlanta, Texas

le 20 Janvier 1896

ayant rempli toutes les conditions imposées par la F.A.I. a été breveté:

Pilote-Aviateur

à la date du 15 Juin 1921

Commission Sportive Aéronautique.

Le Président:

Signature du Titulaire

Bessie Coleman

N°. *Du Brevet:* 18.310.

Certificate from the Federation Aeronautique Internationale, granting Bessie Coleman a pilot's license in France. June 15, 1921.

Photo courtesy of The UT Institute of Texan Cultures at San Antonio

Bessie returned to her home state in 1925. That year she moved to Houston and gave her first Texas air show there on June 19, 1925.

She always refused to participate in any air show that would not let blacks attend. Once, in Waxahachie, she refused to participate unless blacks were allowed to use the same entrance as whites.

In 1926 Bessie moved to Florida where she opened a beauty parlor to supplement her income from the flying and lecture circuits. She was saving money to open a flying school for

African Americans. But that was a goal she would never achieve.

On April 30, 1926, Bessie was thrown from her airplane during a test flight. Her mechanic was flying the craft while she scouted a good landing site for a parachute jump she planned for later that day. Bessie had not fastened her seatbelt and was catapulted from her seat when the plane went into a tailspin. She died on impact. Her mechanic, William Wills, could not regain control of the plane and was killed when it crashed on the airfield. A wrench was discovered stuck in the plane's flight controls.

Bessie was buried in Lincoln Cemetery in Chicago after a funeral in Florida.

The Stinson Sisters Site

The **Stinson Chapter of The Texas Air Museum** maintains a display that includes photos, memorabilia, and an alarmingly rickety looking aircraft that belonged to the sisters.

Hours: 10 A.M. to 4 P.M. Mon.-Sat., 11 A.M. to 4 P.M. Sundays

Admission: $4 adults, $3 senior citizens or members of the military, $2 children 6 to 12, $1 for children younger than 6 or on school tours

Location: In a hangar at the west end of the airfield at Stinson Airport (This is not the big international airport. It is a small municipal airport six miles south of downtown San Antonio.)

Phone Number: 210-977-9885

Address: 8406 Cadmus, San Antonio, TX 78214-3001

Web Address: None

The Lives of the Stinson Sisters

In the early days of American aviation—when any pilot was a novelty and a female pilot was cause for outright amazement—Katherine and Marjorie Stinson claimed a place for themselves in the sky and in the history books. In addition to their individual accomplishments, they operated a flying school in San Antonio and were involved with the now-famous Stinson aircraft business.

But their story begins in Alabama where both were born, Katherine on February 14, 1891, and Marjorie in 1896.

Katherine had musical aspirations and wanted to attend school in Europe so she could become a piano teacher. Air shows were popular at the time, so she hit upon the idea of flying as a way to earn money. Ironically, the family sold its piano to pay for her lessons. In July 1912 she became the fourth woman to get a pilot's license in the United States.

Her petite stature and long curly hair earned her the nickname "The Flying Schoolgirl." She performed in air shows across the country, and music lessons were soon forgotten.

By 1913 the family had moved to Arkansas, and that year Katherine and her mother, Emma Stinson, founded the Stinson Aviation Company in Hot Springs. That same year the family moved to San Antonio, Texas, and soon opened the Stinson School of Flying.

In 1914 eighteen-year-old Marjorie followed her big sister into the skies when she earned her pilot's license on August 12. She was the ninth American woman to get a pilot's license and, at that time, the youngest. She joined her sister as an instructor at the school in San Antonio.

Katherine supervised the construction and repair of airplanes and managed the airfield at the school while honing her skills and continuing to perform as a stunt pilot. She became famous for performing aerial acrobatics at night in a biplane with flares affixed to its wings, and she was the first

Katherine Stinson, circa 1910
Photo courtesy of The UT Institute of Texan Cultures at San Antonio,
The San Antonio Light Collection.

Majorie Stinson is sworn in as an airmail pilot by George Armistead, San Antonio postmaster at Fort Sam Houston, Texas on May 4, 1915. Following the ceremony, Majorie flew a pouch of mail to a flying exhibition in Seguin, where she dropped the mail from her Wright biplane so that it landed in front of the post office.

Photo by W.D.

The UT Institute of Texan Cultures at San Antonio,
The San Antonio Express-News.

person—male or female—to perform a snap roll at the top of a loop (a feat she accomplished in a plane she built herself).

In 1916 she became the first woman to fly in the Far East, and fan clubs sprang up across Japan and China in her honor. In 1917 she set a long-distance record when she flew the 610 miles between San Diego and San Francisco by herself, and she later bested that record with a 783-mile flight between Chicago and New York.

The flying school closed in 1917 thanks to war shortages. By then Katherine and Marjorie had trained many Canadians who went on to fly in World War I.

In 1918 Marjorie became the first woman certified as an air mail pilot for the U.S. Postal Service.

By that time the United States was involved in World War I, and Katherine wanted to fly for her country. She was rejected because of gender. She went to Europe anyway and drove an ambulance for the Red Cross. While there she contracted tuberculosis, and the disease ended her flying career.

After the war she moved to New Mexico, became an architect, and married pilot Miguel Otero Jr. Katherine died on July 8, 1977, in Santa Fe at the age of eighty-six and was buried in Santa Fe National Cemetery.

Marjorie continued to fly, performing across the country at fairs and air shows. In 1929 she was among ninety-nine women who formed the Ninety-Nines, an organization for women pilots that is still thriving today. She quit flying professionally in 1930 and moved to Washington, D.C., where she worked as a draftsman for the U.S. War Department for fifteen years. She retired from that job in 1945. For the next thirty years she devoted much of her time to researching and writing about aviation.

Marjorie died at age seventy-nine in 1975, and her ashes were scattered over Stinson Field in San Antonio.

Women Airforce Service Pilots Sites

The WASP trained at **Avenger Field** in Sweetwater. Today part of that site is a municipal airport of the same name, and the rest is occupied by Texas State Technical College. The college maintains two WASP sites. One is a small metal building that looks like a mini aircraft hangar. Inside are photographs,

WASP trainees prepare to toss a pal into the wishing well at Avenger Field.
Photo courtesy of The Woman's Collection, TWU

articles, and scrapbooks filled with information about the WASP. Across the street is a **wishing well** that was there when the WASP trained at Avenger. When one of the pilots successfully completed a solo flight, her pals would seize her and toss her into the fountain. A bronze statue of a WASP in flight gear now stands sentinel in the middle of the wishing well. The path that leads to the fountain is called the Walk of Honor. The names of all WASP trainees are inscribed on polished stone slabs that flank the path. The gold stars by some names indicate casualties.

Find out more about the WASP at www.wasp-wwii.org.

Avenger Field today

Hours: No set hours. The entire display is outdoors.
Admission: None
Location: Take exit 240 off I-20 and take Spur 170 to the
      north. It's a bit confusing, so go slow and watch for
      signs to the college. Turn into the college campus and
      stay to the right. The college buildings will be on your
      left and the airstrip on the right. You can't miss the
      little metal WASP building. It is topped with a render-
      ing of Fifinella, the Disney-designed WASP mascot
      that looks a bit like a fairy in an old-fashioned aviator
      cap and goggles. There is also a flagpole out front.
      The wishing well is across the street.
Phone Number: 800-592-8784 for TSTC
Address: 300 College Drive, Sweetwater, TX 79556
Web Address: None

There is a bronze statue of the Walt Disney-created and trade-marked WASP mascot, Fifinella, in the foyer of the **Nolan County Courthouse** on the town square.

The wishing well as it looks today

Hours: 9 A.M. to 5 P.M., Mon-Fri.
Admission: None
Location: Downtown Sweetwater
Phone Number: 915-235-5488 for the Sweetwater Chamber of Commerce
Address: 100 E. 3rd Street, Sweetwater, TX 79556
Web Address: None

A WASP room in Sweetwater's **City-County Pioneer Museum** displays artifacts including photos, old periodicals, uniforms, log books, and other items used by the WASP trainees.

Hours: 1 to 5 P.M., Tues.-Sat. Closed holidays
Admission: Free
Location: In a restored, tree-shaded historic house a few
    blocks east of the Nolan County Courthouse in central
    Sweetwater, one block north of Broadway Street
Phone Number: 915-235-8547
Address: 610 E. 3rd Street, Sweetwater, TX 79556
Web Address: http://camalott.com/~sweetwater/
    museum.html

Not far from Sweetwater, six miles southwest of the little town
of Merkel, is a **historical marker** near the spot where
Cornelia Clark Fort died in a crash while on a mission for the
Women's Auxiliary Ferrying Squadron, the precursor to the
WASP. Cornelia was the first woman pilot to die in the line of
duty while flying an American military aircraft. Her plane col-
lided with another craft during a cross-country flight and
crashed on March 21, 1943. The marker is at the intersection of
FM 1085 and FM 126. Merkel is about 20 miles west of Abilene
along Interstate 20. To get to the marker, take the exit for
FM 126 from I-20 and go south to where it intersects with
FM 1085.

Texas Woman's University in Denton maintains the
WASP Archive on the second floor of the Blagg-Huey
Library. There is a bronze statue of a woman flyer in the second-floor foyer and a display of WASP memorabilia including
uniforms, logbooks, and photos in a small research room. The
papers in the WASP Archives are available to researchers by
appointment. (Keep in mind that this is first and most impor-
tantly a place for learning, not a tourist attraction.)

Hours: 8 A.M. to 5 P.M., Mon.-Fri.
Admission: Free
Location: Second floor of the Blagg-Huey Library on the
    TWU main campus in Denton. Drive through the main

entrance; get a parking pass and park on the right. The library is easy to spot as you drive through the main entrance: Just look for the building with the small white dome.

Phone Number: 940-898-3751

Address: P.O. Box 425528, Denton, TX 76204

Web Address: www.twu.edu/library/womans/womansc/ wasp.htm

The **Frontiers of Flight Museum** in Dallas maintains a WASP collection and a display about other women in aviation. Many WASP were stationed at Love Field during World War II. Their commander, Florene Miller Watson, says that she was once ordered to keep track of her pilots' menstrual cycles and ground the gals who were having their periods. It was a short-lived experiment, and there is no record of any menstrual-induced plane crashes among the WASP. There has been talk of moving this museum, but for now its home is at Love Field.

Hours: 10 A.M. to 5 P.M. Mon.-Sat.; 1 to 5 P.M. Sundays

Admission: $3 adults, $1.50 children younger than 12

Location: Second level of the Love Field terminal building. North of downtown Dallas, this is not DFW International Airport. It is a smaller though quite busy regional airport. From Interstate 35, take exit 433 B and go east on Mockingbird Lane. There will be signs for Love Field. The airport is at the intersection of Mockingbird Lane and Cedar Springs Road. Rush hour traffic is horrendous in this area, so plan your visit with that in mind.

Phone Number: 214-350-1651

Address: 8008 Cedar Springs Road, Love Field Terminal LB-18, Dallas, TX 75235

Web Address: www.flightmuseum.org/ (The Web site incorrectly lists the WASP as Women's Army Service Pilots.)

The **American Heritage Airpower Museum** in Midland has a WASP display among its excellent collection.

Hours: 9 A.M. to 5 P.M. Mon.-Sat., noon to 5 P.M. Sundays and holidays, closed Thanksgiving and Christmas Day

Admission: $7 adults, $6 teens (13-18) and senior citizens (65+), $5 children 6-12, free for children under 5 and members of the museum and the Confederate Air Force. Discounts offered for membership in a variety of organizations. Group rates are available but tours must be scheduled in advance.

Location: On the grounds of the Midland International Airport. It is a separate facility, not part of the main terminal building. The way is well marked and it is easy to find.

Phone Number: 915-563-1000

Address: 9600 Wright Drive, Midland, TX 79711

Web Address: www.airpowermuseum.org/

The Life of the Women Airforce Service Pilots

It's common knowledge that women marched into the factories during World War II, but how many people know that women also climbed into the cockpits of American military planes during that time?

In all, 1,101 women became civilian pilots for the military during World War II, freeing male fliers for overseas duty. Between September 1942 and December 1944, 1,074 women served in the Women Airforce Service Pilots (WASP), and 25 with the Women Auxiliary Ferrying Service (WAFS), which was the precursor to the WASP.

They flew every type of aircraft the U.S. military had— trainers, transports, fighters, and bombers. They were the first women in American history hired to fly for the United States military.

In 1943 the WASP and the WAFS merged under the command of Jacqueline Cochran. WASP pilots first trained at

Howard Hughes Field in Houston, but the crowded airspace and lack of facilities prompted a move to Avenger Field in Sweetwater. Avenger was quickly dubbed "Cochran's Convent" because of a no-dating rule. But that didn't keep the men away. The female flyers were a curiosity, and many planes with male crews reported mysterious engine problems that "forced" them to land at Avenger Field.

Conditions in Sweetwater were harsh. The barracks were one board thick with no insulation and did little to protect the women from the heat. And in Sweetwater it gets *very* hot. To escape the heat the women often dragged their cots outside to sleep between the barracks. But they had to watch out for rattlesnakes. The crawly critters were a constant menace, getting into everything including the airplanes.

Aggravations weren't limited to local wildlife. The trainees were given Army-issue mechanic's overalls for daily wear—nothing smaller than a size 44. They had to roll up the cuffs and cinch the waists. The women called them "zoot suits." The planes they flew were also "too big" for many of the women, so they stacked parachute fanny packs on the seats in order to see.

The women went through the same six-month training program as the men, completing ground school, basic flight training, and advanced flight training.

After graduation the women went to bases throughout the United States, earning $50 a month less than their male counterparts. At first they only ferried planes, but by late 1943 their duties had expanded to include transporting people and cargo, training other pilots (including men), and towing targets for artillery practice. (The soldiers practiced with live ammunition and sometimes hit the planes instead of the targets.) One woman even became a test pilot at Wright Patterson Air Base in Ohio.

Two WASPs got to fly the B-29 bomber as part of a stunt to shame male aviators who feared the new plane. The day after Dora Strother and Dorothea "Doro" Johnson Moorman flew their first B-29 mission, an officer at the Clovis, N.M. base issued a memo referring to them as "the two luscious femmes." He wrote that flying the bomber was "quite a job for two delicate dishes of femininity." The note concluded: "Perhaps they should take some of our supermen for a ride and show them how to get off the ground with speed and dispatch."

The ploy worked. Although the initial crews that flew with Dora and Doro refused to take off their parachutes during flights, it took only three weeks for enough men to volunteer for B-29 duty. The WASP pilots were removed from the cockpit and never flew the Superfortress again.

Thirty-eight of the women flyers died on duty during World War II—twenty-seven on active duty and eleven in training. There was no government provision for sending home the bodies for burial; the other women pilots usually took up a collection.

By the spring of 1944 the pilot shortage was over. That put many civilian male pilots at risk of being drafted into the ground troops—unless they could get the women pilots' jobs. At that time Congress was considering a bill that would have given the WASP official military status, so the male pilots launched a massive anti-WASP campaign. The lobby succeeded, and the bill failed. Some of the WASP pilots offered to continue flying for free but were turned down.

The WAFS and WASP were disbanded on December 20, 1944. It would be more than three decades before women were allowed to fly military aircraft for the United States again. In the mid-1970s the WASP mobilized after the Pentagon announced the U.S. Air Force would be training the first ten women ever to fly U.S. military aircraft.

The WASP had been the first, and they wanted everyone to know it.

In 1977, thirty-three years after the WASP flew their final missions, Congress finally granted them military status. The

WASP Commander Jackie Cochran
Photo courtesy The Woman's Collection, Texas Woman's University

surviving WASP continue to meet every other year for a reunion. In 2000 they gathered in Sweetwater and helped dedicate the WASP sites at Avenger Field and in Merkel. For many, the highlight of the weekend was standing at attention while a B-1 bomber with an all-female crew flew overhead and waggled its wings at them.

Other Places and Their People

· Jefferson, Texas ·

Jefferson is a little town snuggled up against Big Cypress Bayou in far East Texas. Founded in 1845 as a river port, it thrived on the business brought by riverboats—the boats came up the Red River, crossed Caddo Lake, and moored in the bayou. The population swelled to 35,000 after the Civil War. (Compare that to the 2,100 people who call it home today.)

Then in 1873 the U.S. government stepped in to clear the Red River and blew up a logjam that kept the waters in Caddo Lake deep enough for steamboats. With the logjam gone, waters levels dropped in the lake and steamboats could no longer navigate it safely. No boats, no business. No business, no people. The population plummeted to about 3,000 residents.

By 1940 the town was a sleepy little backwater with a plethora of shabby, historic buildings including the Excelsior House Hotel. That year the recently formed Jesse Allen Wise Garden Club organized a Dogwood Trail tour in Jefferson, which morphed into a tour of historic homes within three years. In 1950 the name of the tour was officially changed to The Jefferson Historical Pilgrimage—the name it still bears today.

The club was making so much money from the annual spring tour that members decided to branch out into historic preservation. First, in 1950, they bought an old abandoned railroad car and outfitted it as a museum. The following year they bought a home called the Presbyterian Manse, restored it, and included it in the spring tour.

In 1961 the Excelsior House Hotel went on the block to pay off debts. Club members feared an outside owner would not appreciate the historic property, so they formed the Jefferson Historical Restoration and Preservation Corporation and bought it themselves. It was in sorry shape. A headline in the

November 19, 1961 *Dallas Morning News* proclaimed: "Clubwomen Tackle Man-Size Job." The following year the refurbished hotel garnered great acclaim. In the fifty-plus years of its existence, the club has bought and restored many historic properties in Jefferson.

Stroll through the town's historic district and look around. Regardless of what you're looking at, it's likely the members of the Jesse Allen Wise Garden Club had something to do with saving it. They sparked—and indeed, maintain—the drive that has made Jefferson a popular destination.

Jefferson is the town that riverboats built—and a ladies' garden club saved.

The Jesse Wise Garden Club still owns the **Excelsior House Hotel**, which counts Ulysses S. Grant, Oscar Wilde, and Lady Bird Johnson among its customers. Tours are offered.

The Excelsior House Hotel

Hours: It's a hotel—it's always open. Check with the
hotel for tour times, which vary.
Admission: Room rates vary. Check with the hotel.
Rooms book far in advance for popular events like the
Jefferson Historical Pilgrimage, so plan early if you
want to stay there.
Location: Take U.S. Highway 59 north from Marshall.
Once in Jefferson, follow the signs to the historic dis-
trict. It's easy to find.
Phone Number: 903-665-2513
Address: 211 W. Austin, Jefferson, TX 75657
Web Address: http://www.theexcelsiorhouse.com/

Every spring the Jefferson Playhouse stages a dramatization of
the **Diamond Bessie Murder Trial**, one of the most notorious
cases in the history of Texas courtrooms. (And this is Texas,
mind you, so that's saying a good deal!)

For information about tickets to the dramatization, write or
call:

Diamond Bessie
P.O. Box 301
Jefferson, TX 75657
903-665-2704

To visit Bessie's grave in **Oakwood Cemetery**: From the historic district, take State Highway 49 to Alley Street (it's not far)
and turn right. (The turn is across the street from a Brookshire
Brothers.) Proceed down Alley Street, across the railroad
tracks. Take the first right after the tracks, near a water tower
emblazoned "Jefferson Bulldogs." That will take you right into
the cemetery. Stay on the main cemetery road until it dead
ends, then turn right. The grave will be on the right, surrounded by a black wrought iron fence.

Diamond Bessie

The woman who would go down in Texas history as Diamond Bessie was born Annie Stone in Syracuse, New York, in 1854. According to some accounts, she became the mistress of a man whose last name was Moore when she was fifteen. Bessie didn't keep the man, but she did keep his name.

It is believed she was working as a prostitute when she met Abraham Rothschild of Cincinnati, a traveling salesman for his father's jewelry business.

On January 19, 1877, the well-dressed couple arrived in Jefferson and registered at the Brooks House as "A. Monroe and wife." It is unknown whether they actually were married, but the predominant belief says "no."

During the next two days they were seen around town, frequently arguing. He was overheard calling her "Bessie."

Rothschild bought a picnic lunch for two the next morning and was seen disappearing into the fog as he walked with Bessie along a footbridge across Big Cypress Creek. He returned to town that afternoon by another path and was seen casually going about his affairs around town. When asked about his wife, he said she was visiting friends and would meet him Tuesday morning to leave town. But on Tuesday morning the staff of the Brooks House found his room empty. Witnesses later stated that Rothschild had left town alone on Tuesday morning on the eastbound train with the couple's luggage.

About a week later a local woman named Sarah King was collecting firewood when she found the body of a well-dressed woman shot in the head. The remnants of a picnic lunch were found nearby. The woman's diamonds and other jewelry were nowhere to be found.

Jefferson residents took up a collection to bury the woman, and an arrest warrant was issued for "A. Monroe" on suspicion of murder. When the authorities discovered that he and the woman had registered as "A. Rothschild and wife from Cincinnati, Ohio," at a hotel in Marshall before arriving in

Jefferson, a new warrant was issued for Abraham Rothschild of Cincinnati, and the victim was identified as Bessie Moore.

Back in Cincinnati, a distraught Rothschild tried to kill himself but succeeded only in blinding himself in the right eye. While still in the hospital, he was arrested and extradition procedures started. He fought extradition but lost on March 19 and was returned to Jefferson to be tried in a case that would take two-and-a-half years to resolve.

The trial was already high profile by the time it began in December 1878. The governor had intervened to choose the prosecutors, and newspapers published florid accounts of every aspect of the case. After three weeks of testimony, the jury found Rothschild guilty of murder in the first degree and sentenced him to death by hanging. Legend has it that jury foreman C. R. Weathersby drew a noose on the wall, signed it, and stated that that was his verdict.

The defense, of course, appealed. The appellate judge overturned the verdict, saying the trial had been unfair and the first court had been in error in allowing a man who stated that he had an opinion about the case to serve on the jury.

Rothschild was indicted again on December 2, 1880, and the second trial began on December 14 in Jefferson. The defense focused on the testimony of Isabelle Gouldy, one of the women who had prepared the body of the victim for burial. She claimed to have seen Bessie with a man who was not the defendant. Rothschild's lawyers also argued that the body was too well preserved to have been in the woods for fifteen days. The jury bought it and acquitted Rothschild on December 30, 1880.

The rumor mill went into hyper drive: It was said that the jury had been bribed and that all twelve jurors died violently within a year of the trial; that Bessie was pregnant at the time of her death; that Rothschild later served time in jail for theft.

One of the most enduring legends is that of an old man wearing an eye patch, who supposedly showed up in Jefferson in the 1890s and asked for directions to the grave of Bessie Moore. He allegedly laid roses on it, prayed, and paid the caretaker to maintain the grave. Was it Abe Rothschild? Or just a Jefferson resident with an active imagination?

In the 1930s a headstone mysteriously appeared on the grave, but a local man later admitted to buying the stone out of sympathy for the victim. In the 1960s the Jessie Allen Wise Garden Club built an iron fence around the grave. The case is still listed as unsolved.

Diamond Bessie is buried in Oakwood Cemetery in Jefferson.

· Johnson Space Center ·

Some women aren't satisfied with reaching for the stars—they want to get out there and visit them. America has been sending people into space since 1961, but it wasn't until 1983 that the first American woman hitched a ride on a rocket. **Dr. Sally Ride** opened that hatch for other women to follow: **Mae Jemison**, the first African American woman in space; **Ellen Ochoa**, the first Hispanic woman in space; space-endurance champ **Shannon Lucid**; and **Eileen Collins**, the first woman space shuttle commander. As of March 1, 2001, thirty-seven American women had flown in space. And at some point, each worked at Johnson Space Center in Houston. Visit **Space Center Houston,** Johnson Space Center's official visitor center, to learn more about women's contributions to the space program or to tour Johnson Space Center. Tip: Get there first thing in the morning to avoid the crowds.

Hours: Summer—9 A.M. to 7 P.M. daily
   Winter—10 A.M. to 5 P.M. Mon.-Fri.,
   10 A.M. to 7 P.M. Sat.-Sun.

Admission: $14.95 adults, $13.95 senior citizens, $10.95
   children 4-11. Group rates available. Note: There is a
   $3 parking fee.

Location: Approximately twenty-five miles south of downtown Houston. From Houston, take Interstate 45
   south toward Galveston. Take Exit 25, turn left (east)
   and proceed three miles down NASA Road 1. The
   center will be on your left.

Phone Number: 281-244-2100

Address: 1601 NASA Road 1, Houston, TX 77058

Web Address: www.jsc.nasa.gov/

Sally Ride

Sally Ride was born May 26, 1951, in Los Angeles, California. She graduated from Westlake High School in 1968 and received bachelors' degrees in physics and English in 1973 from Stanford University. She got her master's and doctoral degrees in physics from Stanford in 1975 and 1978, respectively.

The same year she received her Ph.D., Sally got the word she'd been waiting for: She was selected for astronaut training. She reported for duty that July. As part of her training, she was a member of the support crew for the second and third space shuttle flights.

Sally made history on June 18, 1983, when she became only the second woman and the first American woman to fly in space. (Soviet cosmonaut Valentina Tereshkova blasted into space in 1963.) As part of the space shuttle *Challenger's* five-member crew, she helped deploy communications satellites for Canada and Indonesia, perform the first satellite deployment and retrieval with the shuttle's robot arm, and

Sally Ride was the first American woman in space.

Photo courtesy of NASA

conduct pharmaceutical and materials research. The shuttle orbited for six days before returning to earth at Edwards Air Force Base in California on June 24, 1983.

She reunited with *Challenger* in October 1984 for her second mission. Over eight days the crew deployed the Earth Radiation Budget satellite, conducted scientific observations of Earth, and demonstrated the potential for satellite refueling by astronauts. The mission lasted 197 hours and concluded with a landing at the Kennedy Space Center in Florida.

Sally was in training for a third mission, when the *Challenger* exploded shortly after take-off in 1986. All flights were suspended. For the next six months, Sally served as a member of the presidential commission investigating the accident. Upon completion of the investigation, she was assigned to NASA headquarters in Washington, D.C. as assistant to the NASA Administrator for long-range planning. In this role she created NASA's Office of Exploration and produced a report on the future of the space program called *Leadership and America's Future in Space*.

She retired from NASA to go back to the classroom. She is now a physics professor at the University of California–San Diego. She also serves on the President's Committee of Advisors on Science and Technology.

Mae Jemison

Dr. Mae C. Jemison blasted into orbit—and the history books—aboard the space shuttle *Endeavor* on September 12, 1992. She was the first African American woman to go into space.

Born in Decatur, Alabama, on October 17, 1956, Mae was the youngest of three children. The family moved to Chicago when she was three.

Astronaut Mae C. Jemison, mission specialist, works in zero gravity in the Science Module aboard the Earth-orbiting Space Shuttle *Endeavour*. Making her first flight in space, Dr. Jemison was joined by five other NASA astronauts and a Japanese payload specialist for eight days of research in support of the Spacelab-J mission, a joint effort between Japan and the United States.
Photo courtesy of NASA

Mae was a good student who showed an early interest in science. When she was sixteen, she won a scholarship to Stanford University, where she studied chemical engineering and African and Afro-American studies. She graduated with a bachelor of science degree in 1977. Then it was on to Cornell Medical College. While there, she indulged a longtime interest in health issues affecting Third World countries. She traveled to Kenya and also served a medical clerkship in Thailand at a Cambodian refugee camp. Mae got her medical degree in 1981 and completed her internship at Los Angeles County/USC Medical Center in 1982.

From 1983 to 1985 Mae served as a medical officer with the Peace Corps in Sierra Leone and Liberia in West Africa. Afterward she returned to Los Angeles and went into private practice.

NASA chose Dr. Jemison for the astronaut corps in 1987. During her mission in 1992 she paid homage to Nichelle Nichols, who played Lt. Uhura on the original "Star Trek" series, saying it had been exciting to see a black woman on TV in a major role. As part of the shuttle crew, Mae conducted experiments in life sciences and material sciences and was co-investigator in a bone cell research experiment.

Mae left NASA in March 1993 and founded The Jemison Group, Inc. in Houston to research, develop, and implement advanced technologies suited to the social, political, cultural, and economic context of the individual, especially in the developing world.

Ellen Ochoa

Ellen Ochoa was born May 10, 1958, in Los Angeles. She graduated from Grossmont High School in La Mesa, California, in 1975 and got her bachelor's degree in physics from San Diego State University in 1980. She went on to study electrical engineering at Stanford University, where she received a master's degree in 1981 and a doctoral degree in 1985.

As a doctoral student at Stanford and later as a researcher at Sandia National Laboratories and NASA Ames Research Center, Ellen investigated optical systems for performing information processing. She is a co-inventor on three patents for an optical inspection system, an optical object recognition method, and a method for noise removal in images. As chief of the Intelligent Systems Technology Branch at Ames, she supervised thirty-five engineers and scientists in the research

Astronaut Ellen Ochoa, mission specialist, takes a brief time out from a busy day in space to play a 15-minute set of flute offerings on the Space Shuttle *Discovery*'s aft flight deck. Ochoa, who has played the flute for 25 years, performed the "Marine Corps Hymn," "Navy Hymn," and "God Save the Queen" for fellow crew members as well as some Vivaldi for herself.

Photo courtesy of NASA

and development of computational systems for aerospace missions.

Ellen is married to Coe Fulmer Miles, and they have one son.

Selected by NASA in January 1990, Ellen became an astronaut in July 1991. Her technical assignments were flight software verification; crew representative for flight software and computer hardware development; crew representative for robotics development, testing, and training; and spacecraft communicator in Mission Control.

On April 8, 1993, Ellen became the first Hispanic woman in space. During a nine-day mission she used a remote manipulator system to deploy and capture a satellite.

The following year she was the payload commander on an eleven-day flight, and in 1999 she was a specialist on a ten-day mission during which the crew performed the first docking to the International Space Station and delivered four tons of logistics and supplies in preparation for the arrival of the station's first crew.

So far, Ellen has logged more than 719 hours in space, and she is assigned as a flight engineer on a ten-day mission to the International Space Station, scheduled for launch in early 2002.

Shannon Lucid

As of 2001, Shannon Lucid holds the international records for most flight hours in orbit by a woman, and by a non-Russian of either gender.

Following a year of training in Star City, Russia, Shannon boarded the space shuttle *Atlantis* and headed for the now-defunct Mir Space Station on March 22, 1996. She stayed on the station for six months, conducting life science and physical science experiments. She ran every day on a treadmill to decrease the amount of muscle and bone loss she was certain to experience in space.

Shannon returned to Earth on September 26, 1996, having spent more time in orbit than any other American in history.

She was born on January 14, 1943, in Shanghai, China, but considers Bethany, Oklahoma, home now. Shannon graduated from Bethany High School in 1960 then went to the University of Oklahoma, where she got a bachelor's degree in chemistry in 1963, a master's in biochemistry in 1970, and a doctoral degree in biochemistry in 1973.

In 1974 Shannon took a job as a research associate with the Oklahoma Medical Research Foundation in Oklahoma City. She worked there until NASA chose her for the astronaut candidate training program in January 1978. She became an astronaut in August 1979. As of 2001, she had flown on five missions.

Her first time in space was in June of 1985 aboard the space shuttle *Discovery*. The crew deployed communications satellites for Mexico, the Arab League, and the United States. They deployed and retrieved another satellite and completed a number of science experiments.

During another flight, which lasted fourteen days in the fall of 1993, the crew performed neurovestibular, cardiovascular, cardiopulmonary, metabolic, and musculoskeletal medical experiments on themselves and forty-eight rats to expand existing knowledge about human and animal physiology on Earth and in space flight.

When she's not working, Shannon likes flying, camping, hiking, reading, and spending time with her husband, Michael Lucid, their daughter, and two sons.

Shannon was recently awarded the Congressional Space Medal of Honor by the president of the United States—the only woman so far to receive it. She was also awarded the Order of Friendship Medal by Russian President Boris Yeltsin, one of the highest Russian civilian awards and the highest award that can be presented to a non-citizen.

Eileen Collins

Eileen Collins was the first woman to pilot a space shuttle and, later, the first woman to command a space shuttle mission.

Born November 19, 1956, in Elmira, New York, Eileen grew up as "a very ordinary person, a down-to-earth individual," according to her parents.

During high school she says she began "reading voraciously about famous pilots, from Amelia Earhart to Women Airforce Service Pilots who played an important role in WWII. Their stores inspired me. I admired the courage of these women to go and fly into dangerous situations!"

She graduated from Elmira Free Academy in 1974 and received an associate degree in mathematics/science from Corning Community College in 1976.

By 1977 Eileen had saved enough money to earn a pilot's license. The following year she graduated from Syracuse University with a bachelor of arts degree in mathematics and economics.

With good grades, flying experience, and a letter of recommendation from her ROTC supervisor, she became one of the first women to go straight from college into Air Force pilot training.

Eileen graduated from Air Force Undergraduate Pilot Training in 1979 and was stationed at Vance AFB, Oklahoma, where she was a T-38 instructor pilot until 1982. From 1983 to 1985 she was a C-141 aircraft commander and instructor pilot at Travis AFB, California. Eileen spent the following year as a student with the Air Force Institute of Technology. From 1986 to 1989 she was assigned to the U.S. Air Force Academy in Colorado, where she was an assistant professor in mathematics and a T-41 instructor pilot. In 1986 she got a master's degree in operations research from Stanford University, and a master of

Astronaut Eileen M. Collins, mission commander, loads a roll of film into
a still camera on Space Shuttle *Columbia*'s middeck. Collins is the first
woman mission commander in the history of human space flight.

Photo courtesy of NASA

arts degree in space systems management from Webster University followed in 1989.

Eileen was tapped by NASA for the astronaut training program while attending the Air Force Test Pilot School at Edwards AFB, California, from which she graduated in 1990.

She became an astronaut in July 1991 and was initially assigned to Orbiter engineering support. A variety of other duties followed. Then, on February 3, 1995, she made her first trip into space, as pilot of the first flight of the new joint Russian-American Space Program. She was the first woman ever to pilot a space shuttle. Her second mission was in May of 1997.

In July of 1999 Eileen became the first woman to command a shuttle mission. During the four-day flight the crew deployed the Chandra X-Ray Observatory.

In addition to the space shuttle, she has flown more than thirty different aircraft, logging more than 5,000 flight hours.

She is married to Pat Youngs, and they have two children.

· Miss Hattie's Bordello Museum ·

How much more "women's history" can you get than a bordello museum? Miss Hattie's in San Angelo is the real deal, too—a former "gentleman's social center" that operated for more than fifty years before the Texas Rangers finally shut it down in 1946. Miss Hattie's was just one of many such establishments in San Angelo at the time, but it was by far the swankiest. Why, Miss Hattie's reportedly had the finest indoor plumbing in *all* of San Angelo. The building's first floor was a saloon while the real business of the place was conducted upstairs. Today it's that second floor that has been turned into a museum, complete with furnishings, memorabilia from Miss Hattie's, and clothing that belonged to the working girls.

Hours: 1 to 4 P.M., Thurs.-Sat. Guided tours only, on the hour

Admission: $5 per head, free for toddlers and infants
   Buy tickets next door at Legend Jewelers

Location: San Angelo's historic district. Take U.S. Highway 67 to San Angelo. Take the Chadbourne Street exit and go south. You'll go through a warehouse district and the road takes two sharp turns, but stay on Chadbourne Street. Turn left onto Concho Street. The museum's sign can be hard to see. Look for the building with the white ceramic brick front.

Phone Number: 915-653-0112 (This is the number for Legend Jewelers, which shares an owner with Miss Hattie's.)

Address: 18½ E. Concho Street, San Angelo, TX 79603

Web Address: None

· Museum of the Gulf Coast ·

This little museum is a jewel tucked away in Port Arthur. The museum staff is serious about including the accomplishments of women among its celebration of local culture. In addition to a big collection of Janis Joplin memorabilia (see the section on Janis for more about that), it offers displays on many successful hometown gals, including:

Barbara Jacket—One of the most successful coaches Texas has ever produced, Barbara was born in Port Arthur in 1935. She and her two siblings were raised by their mother. Barbara attended Lincoln High School, where she was a basketball and track star. She graduated in 1954 and went on to college at the Tuskegee Institute. After earning her college degree in 1958, Barbara began her coaching career at Lincoln High School before taking a job as the women's track coach at Prairie View A&M. In her twenty-seven years at the college, her teams won more than thirty-two titles. She was named Southwestern Athletic Conference Coach of the Year twenty-three times, and National Association of Intercollegiate Athletics Coach of the Year five times. In 1992 she coached the Olympic women's track team to four gold medals, three silver medals, and three bronze medals. She was only the second black woman to coach an Olympic team. Barbara stopped coaching at A&M in 1991 in order to devote more time to Olympic coaching, but she remains the school's athletic director.

Evelyn Keyes—Born in 1916, Evelyn was an actress whose most famous role was as Scarlett O'Hara's younger sister, Suellen, in *Gone With the Wind*. She appeared in forty-seven feature-length films, including *The Seven Year Itch* and *The Jolson Story*. Evelyn also acted on the stage, did guest-appearances on many television shows, and published several stories.

Thelma "Tad" Tadlock—Born in Port Arthur in 1931, Tad knew she wanted to be a dancer by the time she was five years old. Her father wanted her to attend college after her graduation from Thomas Jefferson High School in 1949, but Tad longed for the excitement of New York City. She made a deal with him: Give me a year; if I strike out, I'll return to Texas and college. She got work in four consecutive plays. In 1959 she started working in television and soon became a featured dancer on the *Hit Parade*. She later joined the *Arthur Murray Dance Party* as a dancer and assistant choreographer. In the course of her career she choreographed for projects ranging from the Miss USA pageant to the movie *Body Heat*.

Hours: 9 A.M. to 5 P.M., Mon.-Sat., 1 to 5 P.M. Sundays

Admission: $3.50 adults, $3 senior citizens, $1.50 children 6 to 18, 50 cents children under 6

Location: These exhibits are scattered throughout the museum. To get to there, take Highway 69 south from Beaumont. Drive all the way through Port Arthur to Procter Street. Take a right and drive past Lamar State College. Turn left on Beaumont Avenue, then take the first left into the museum parking lot. It is across the street from the City of Port Arthur Police Department.

Phone Number: 409-982-7000

Address: 700 Procter, Port Arthur, TX 77640

Web Address: www.pa.lamar.edu/museum/gulf.html

· National Cowgirl Hall of Fame ·

The National Cowgirl Hall of Fame is moving to Fort Worth from Hereford, Texas, where it was founded in 1975 to "honor and document the lives of women who have distinguished themselves while exemplifying the pioneer spirit of the American West." Honorees include everyone from Texas Rose Bascom, Dale Evans, and Laura Ingalls Wilder to Texas's own Hallie Stillwell and Henrietta King. The hall's artifacts are in storage while a new 33,000-square-foot building is constructed in Fort Worth. It is slated to open in 2002.

Hours: To be determined
Admission: To be determined
Location: Downtown Fort Worth at the intersection of Gendy and Burnett-Tandy Streets.
Phone Number: 817-336-4475, 800-476-FAME
Address: 111 West 4th Street, Suite 300, Fort Worth, TX 76102 (Note: This is the address for the museum offices during the construction.)
Web Address: www.cowgirl.net

· Texas Black Woman's Archives ·

The Texas Black Woman's Archives at the African American History Museum at Fair Park in Dallas offers resources about the history and experiences of black women. Exhibits rotate.

Hours: Noon to 5 P.M. Tues.-Fri., 10 A.M. to 5 P.M. Saturdays, 1 to 5 P.M. Sundays

Admission: Free

Location: Ten minutes east of downtown Dallas (depending on traffic). Take Interstate 30 east from downtown and follow the signs to Fair Park. (Look for the big Ferris wheel; it's always there, even when the state fair is not in session.) Signs inside the park will get you to the museum.

Phone Number: 214-565-9026

Address: 3536 Grand Avenue, Dallas, TX 75210-1005

Web Address: None

· Texas Woman's University ·

An eleven-year grassroots movement culminated in 1901 when the state legislature finally approved a state institution of higher learning for women. Denton was selected as the site for this new school in 1902, and it was called Girls' Industrial College. Classes began in 1903 with an enrollment of 186 students and a faculty of fourteen. It was the first educational institution in the state to offer instruction in home economics The name changed to College of Industrial Arts in 1905, to Texas State College for Women in 1934, and to Texas Woman's University in 1957. It was accredited by the American Association of University Women in 1925 and placed on the approved list of the Association of American Universities in 1929. Male students were admitted for the first time in 1972. TWU's mission statement is this: To serve as a resource and depository for information and knowledge about women and their particular contributions to the history and progress of the state of Texas, the nation, and the world.

Just walking around the TWU campus is a pleasure. It's among the loveliest college campuses in the state. Be sure to visit the Little Chapel-in-the-Woods. A popular spot for student weddings, it was dedicated by First Lady Eleanor Roosevelt in 1939. The **Blagg-Huey Library**, with its distinctive dome, is the most recognizable building on campus and houses the university's stellar Woman's Collection, which includes books, manuscripts, photographs, microfilm, and oral histories about the history of women in the United States.

TWU Library
Photo courtesy of Texas Woman's University

Hours: Library hours vary depending on the semester.
The Woman's Collection hours are 8 A.M. to 5 P.M.
Mon.-Fri. Note: This is a research facility, so it's best
to call ahead for an appointment.
Admission: Free
Location: The Woman's Collection is on the second floor
of the library.
Phone Number: 940-898-3751
Address: P.O. Box 425528, Denton, TX 76204
Web Address: www.twu.edu/library/womans/

Don't miss the **DAR Museum** at TWU. It features a permanent exhibit of inaugural gowns of first ladies of the Republic of Texas, the state of Texas, and the United States.

> *Hours*: 8 A.M. to 5 P.M. Mon.-Fri. and occasionally on Saturdays. Guided tours by appointment
> *Admission*: Free
> *Location*: The Administration Conference Tower (commonly called the Clock Tower) in the skybridge that spans Administration Drive
> *Phone Number*: 940-898-2669
> *Address*: 304 Administration Dr., Denton, TX 76201
> *Web Address*: www.twu.edu/twu/exhibits/firstladies/

· The Women's Museum: An Institute for the Future ·

The Women's Museum: An Institute for the Future is an amazing—and amazingly comprehensive—facility that opened at Fair Park in Dallas in 2000. It maintains a collection of artifacts, some of them from the Smithsonian Institution, but its primary focus is on high-tech, interactive displays about women and their accomplishments. Emphasis is on the interactive. It's a great place. If you only have time to go to one women's history site in Texas, this is the one to choose. As you walk toward the front doors, be sure to take a look at the statue that graces the front of the building. The model for it was Dallas teenager Georgia Carroll, who went on to be a supermodel in the 1930s and a big band singer in the late thirties and early forties. She married big band leader Kay Kyser and retired to North Carolina.

Hours: 10 A.M. to 5 P.M. Tues.-Sat., noon to 5 P.M. Sundays

Admission: $5 adults, $4 senior citizens and students 13 to 18, $3 students 5 to 12, free for children younger than 5. Group discounts available.

Location: Ten minutes east of downtown Dallas (depending on traffic). Take Interstate 30 east from downtown and follow the signs to Fair Park. (Look for the big Ferris wheel; it's always there, even when the state fair is not in session.) Signs inside the park will get you to the museum. It's at the corner of Parry Avenue.

The Women's Museum: An Institute for the Future

Photo taken by Bruce Maxwell/Courtesy of the Women's Museum

Phone Number: 214-915-0860, 877-915-0860
Address: 3800 Parry Avenue, Dallas, TX 75226
Web Address: www.thewomensmuseum.org

· Suggested Itineraries ·

Day Trips:

In and Around Dallas/Fort Worth

These destinations are great to visit one at a time, or together as part of a "day of women's history" in the Dallas/Fort Worth area.

- The Eagle Ford School in west Dallas where bad girl Bonnie Parker attended classes *(page 160)*.

- Crown Hill Memorial Cemetery in northwest Dallas where Bonnie Parker is buried *(page 161)*. This is easily combined with a trip to the Frontiers of Flight Museum.

- The Frontiers of Flight Museum at Love Field in north Dallas, which maintains a display on the Women Airforce Service Pilots, many of whom were stationed there during World War II *(page 179)*.

- The Texas Black Woman's History Archives at the African American Museum at Fair Park in central Dallas *(page 207)*. Combine this with a trip to The Women's Museum: An Institute for the Future.

- The Women's Museum: An Institute for the Future, at Fair Park in central Dallas *(page 211)*. Combine this with a visit to the Texas Black Woman's Archives.

- The Mary Kay Museum in Addison, a suburb in north Dallas *(page 25)*. This is easily combined with a trip to the Frontiers of Flight Museum, with a stop for lunch on

"Restaurant Row," a stretch of Beltline Road overflowing with eateries.

🐛 Head south out of Dallas on U.S. Highway 175 to Kemp for a visit to the Kemp Calaboose, where Bonnie Parker spent a night imprisoned with another member of the Barrow Gang *(page 160)*.

🐛 The historical marker at Highway 114 and Dove Road in Grapevine, a small town between Dallas and Fort Worth, is the site of a Bonnie and Clyde gun battle with police *(page 161)*. Combine this with the Eagle Ford School, Crown Hill Memorial Cemetery, and Kemp trips for a Bonnie Parker tour.

🐛 In Denton, a college town about 35 miles north of Dallas and Forth Worth, visit Texas Woman's University *(page 208)*, the first public college for women in the state. While on campus, check out the WASP Archive on the second floor of the Blagg-Huey Library *(page 178)* and visit the DAR Museum of first ladies' dresses in the Administration Building *(page 210)*.

🐛 Follow your nose to the Mrs Baird's Bakery and Corporate Headquarters in south Fort Worth *(page 28)*.

🐛 In central Fort Worth, visit the Physiology Hall of the Museum of Science and History *(page 115)*. Combine this with a trip to the nearby downtown area. (See next.)

🐛 Visit the National Cowgirl Hall of Fame *(page 206)* in downtown Fort Worth. Combine this with seeing the medical school historical marker at 301 Fifth Street *(page 117)*, and with a trip to the nearby Museum of Science and History.

In and Around Houston

These sites are spread out. A day of women's history in the Houston area will require a lot of miles in Houston's infamous traffic. Better to take them one or two at a time.

- A visit to Ima Hogg's gorgeous Bayou Bend in west Houston is worth at least half a day *(page 111)*.

- Make an appointment to see legislator Barbara Jordan's papers at Texas Southern University in central Houston *(page 47)*.

- The Texas Golf Hall of Fame in the north Houston suburb of Spring celebrates many women golfers, including Babe Didrikson Zaharias and the great Betsy Rawls *(page 129)*.

- Visit Space Center Houston, adjacent to the Johnson Space Center, in far south Houston for a glimpse into the experiences of America's women astronauts *(page 192)*.

- About 50 miles northwest of Houston, visit Liendo Plantation in Hempstead where artist Elizabet Ney lived and is buried *(page 101)*.

- Head east on Interstate 10 to Beaumont for a visit to the Babe Didrikson Zaharias Museum and Visitor Center *(page 124)*, and the golfer's grave *(page 126)*. Plan a stop at the San Jacinto Monument and Museum on the way back to Houston *(page 120)*, then debate the existence of the Yellow Rose of Texas over supper at the Monument Inn Restaurant.

- Take a jaunt east to Port Arthur and the Museum of the Gulf Coast *(page 204)*, one of the best small museums in the state. The facility's staff has made a serious effort to include women's contributions in the museum's collection, and the effort shows.

In and Around Austin

Austin is overflowing with women's history—so much, in fact, that it is impossible to visit all these places in a single day.

🐾 The Texas State Capitol in downtown Austin is the site of much women's history and host to a statue of Stephen F. Austin by Elizabet Ney *(page 37)*.

🐾 The former home of Alamo survivor Susanna Dickinson is moving from 501 W. Fifth Street to a permanent central Austin home at Tenth Street and Congress Avenue in 2001 *(pages 5-6)*.

🐾 At Oakwood Cemetery in central Austin, visit the graves of Susanna Dickinson, Annie Blanton, and Ima Hogg *(pages 6, 50, and 112)*.

🐾 Visit Laguna Gloria, the former home of Alamo savior Clara Driscoll, in north Austin *(page 9)*.

🐾 At the Texas State Cemetery in central Austin, visit the graves of Miriam "Ma" Ferguson and Barbara Jordan *(pages 39 and 47)*.

🐾 The Elizabet Ney Museum, in the artist's former studio and home in north Austin, is worth a leisurely visit *(page 101)*.

🐾 On the southwest outskirts of Austin, meander through the multicolored glory of the Lady Bird Johnson Wildflower Center *(page 131)*. This is mostly an outdoor attraction, so plan your visit for a good-weather day.

🐾 At the Lyndon Baines Johnson Library and Museum in central Austin, visit the First Lady's Gallery for an insight into Lady Bird Johnson *(page 134)*.

🐾 Head north on Interstate 35 to Belton for a visit to the home of Sanctificationist leader Martha White McWhirter *(page 143)* and the Bell County Museum *(page 39)* for a glimpse into the life of Miriam Ferguson, Texas's first woman governor.

🐾 South of Austin off Interstate 35 in Kyle, visit the Katherine Anne Porter Literary Center *(page 79)*.

🐾 Austin is a good starting point for all Hill Country trips, including day trips to San Antonio.

In San Antonio

🐾 Visit the Alamo in downtown San Antonio to find out about all the women who survived the famous siege, the one who died, and the gals who saved the mission and turned it into a protected historic landmark *(page 2)*. Combine this with a trip to the Hertzberg Circus Museum.

🐾 The Hertzberg Circus Museum in downtown San Antonio is a nifty place and includes a display on famed Texas circus queen Mollie Bailey *(page 33)*. Combine this with a visit to the Alamo.

🐾 Just north of downtown San Antonio, at the municipal airfield, visit the Stinson Chapter of the Texas Air Museum for an introduction to the amazing Stinson sisters, Katherine and Marjorie *(page 170)*.

🐾 San Antonio is a good starting point for all Hill Country trips, including day trips to Austin.

Multi-day Trips:

Northeast Texas

🐾 Starting from Dallas, take Interstate 20 east to Kilgore and visit the Rangerette Showcase and Museum *(page 52)*. Afterward, get back on the interstate and continue east to Marshall, then go north on U.S. Highway 59 to Jefferson *(page 186)*. Plan to stay at least one night in this charming little town, but be sure to make reservations—especially in the spring when the wildflowers and the re-enactment of the Diamond Bessie murder trial draw hordes of tourists. On your first full day in Jefferson, tour the historic district in the morning, being sure to stop at the Excelsior House Hotel. After lunch, head out to Potter's Point *(page 21)*. On the way back into Jefferson, stop at Diamond Bessie's grave *(page 188)*. While in Jefferson, try to catch a performance at the Living Room Theater, 112 Vale Street. Marcia Thomas—the owner, playwright, actress, and head janitor—specializes in one-woman shows about women. As you leave Jefferson headed south on U.S. Highway 59, take a detour through Karnack to see the childhood home of Lady Bird Johnson *(page 134)*. Then continue to Marshall and Interstate 20 and return to Dallas [2 to 4 days, depending on the length of the stopover in Jefferson].

❦ Starting from Dallas, take Interstate 20 east to U.S. Highway 69, then head north on U.S. Highway 69 to Mineola. Continue north on State Highway 37 to Quitman and visit the Governor Hogg Shrine State Historical Park *(page 109)*. Backtrack to Mineola and visit the birthplace of philanthropist Ima Hogg *(page 109)*. Take a lunch and a camera—it's a great place for a picnic and pictures. Then continue south on U.S. Highway 69 to Tyler for a visit to the Bonner-Whitaker-McClendon House, childhood abode of trailblazing journalist Sarah McClendon *(page 83)*. Stay overnight in Tyler, then head south on State Highway 31 to Athens. Just west of Athens, turn north on U.S. Highway 175 and take a detour through Kemp to see the little jail (emphasis on "little"!) where Bonnie Parker spent a night *(page 160)*. If you have trouble finding it, just ask at the post office or the city hall. Continue north on U.S. 175 into Dallas. If time allows, add one of the Dallas day trips to round out the day. This is a great trip to combine with a tour of Tyler's Azalea Trail in the spring. [2 days]

❦ Combine the Jefferson and Tyler itineraries, then add visits to sites suggested in the Day Trips section for Dallas/Fort Worth to make a full week of touring women's history in northeast Texas. [5 to 7 days]

East Texas

❦ From Dallas, head south on Interstate 35. Stop in Waco for a pre-arranged tour of the Mrs Baird's plant *(page 30)*. Then continue south on the interstate to Belton. (Or skip the Waco stop and go straight to Belton.) In Belton, stop at the Bell County Museum for a look at the lives of Miriam Ferguson *(page 39)*, Texas's first female governor, and fiery Sanctificationist leader Martha White McWhirter *(page 143)*. From the museum, walk the few blocks to McWhirter's house *(page 144)*. Plan to stay overnight in Belton and be sure to see the recently refurbished Bell County Courthouse. It is one of the loveliest courthouses in Texas. Leave Belton, heading north on Interstate 35 to Waco and take State Highway 164 east to Groesbeck. From there, take State Highway 14 north to Old Fort Parker Historical Park for a fascinating look at the spot where Cynthia Ann Parker and others were kidnapped by a band of Native Americans in 1836 *(page 148)*. Plan enough time to view a video about the attack, poke through the cabins, climb the corner blockhouse, and visit the grave where those killed or abducted during the raid are memorialized. Leave the park and continue north on State Highway 14 to U.S. Highway 84. West will take you back to Interstate 35 and east will take you to Interstate 45. [2 days]

❦ The preceding itinerary also makes a great trip from Waco or Austin. From Austin, take Interstate 35 north to begin the trip in Belton. Stop in Waco for the tour of the Mrs Baird's plant, then head to Old Fort Parker Historical Park. When leaving Fort Parker, go south on State Highway 14 to

State Highway 7, then head west to get back to Interstate 35. [2 days]

Southeast Texas

❦ From Houston, take Interstate 10 east, stopping at the San Jacinto Monument and Museum to reflect on the legend of the Yellow Rose of Texas *(page 120)*. Then continue east to Beaumont to visit the Babe Didrikson Zaharias Museum and Visitor Center *(page 124)*. Make time to visit Babe's grave *(page 126)*, then head south to Port Arthur (the way is well marked) and visit the excellent Museum of the Gulf Coast *(page 91)*. When you are through browsing the displays on rock icon Janis Joplin, actress Evelyn Keyes, Olympic coach Barbara Jacket and others, leave Port Arthur via State Highway 87 and push on to Galveston. Plan to stay at least two nights in this island town. Be sure to make reservations, especially during Mardi Gras, spring break, and the wintertime Dickens on the Strand celebration. While in Galveston, visit the homes of musician Olga Samaroff *(page 88)* and political activist and all-around Texas character Minnie Fisher Cunningham *(page 42)*, and plan a quick stop at the Ashbel Smith Building on the University of Texas Medical Branch campus *(page 42)*. Don't miss the Lone Star Flight Museum, which has the only display in the state on pioneering aviator Bessie Coleman *(page 166)*. Return to Houston via Interstate 45 north, with a stop at Space Center Houston *(page 192)*. [3 to 5 days]

❦ From Houston, take U.S. Highway 59 southwest to Richmond and a brief visit with the memory of Jane Long *(page 157)*. Continue west on U.S. Highway 59 to State Highway 36 then head south to visit the Carry Nation historical marker in East Columbia *(page 138)* and Varner-Hogg Plantation in West Columbia *(page 110)*. Leave West Columbia driving north on State Highway 36 to Alternate

U.S. Highway 90. Take it west to Hallettsville. Stay overnight in Hallettsville, then tour the sites dedicated to town founder Margaret Hallett *(page 67)*. Take U.S. Highway 77 north out of Hallettsville, to Interstate 10 and head east, back to Houston, with a stop in Columbus to visit the home and grave of diarist Dilue Rose Harris *(pages 77 and 78)*. Be sure to make a reservation to tour the Dilue Rose Harris House, or you will have to satisfy yourself with a view of its exterior. [2 days]

South Texas

🐾 This is a great trip to take from Houston or San Antonio, or a good add-on to any trip to Corpus Christi. In Corpus Christi, tour all the Selena sites *(pages 94-97)*. This can take one to three days, depending on many places you stop and how long you spend at each one. [1 to 3 days]

🐾 Add a day or two to the preceding trip, and get acquainted with the memory of birder Connie Hagar in Rockport *(page 62)*. From Corpus Christi, head north across Corpus Christi Bay (or from Padre Island take State Highway 361) to Aransas Pass and continue north on State Highway 35 to Rockport. This is an especially good trip to take during the spring and fall bird migrations. Texas Parks & Wildlife monitors the migrations—call 512-389-4800 or visit its website at www.tpwd.state.tx.us/ to time your visit. [2 to 4 days]

🐾 From Corpus Christi, head west on State Highway 44 then south on U.S. Highway 77 to Kingsville for a visit to the famous King Ranch, which was helmed to success by Henrietta King *(page 154)*. Be sure to visit Henrietta's grave in Kingsville. Combine this trip with either of the preceding two trips—or both of them! [2 to 5 days]

The Hill Country

☙ From San Antonio, take Interstate 10 east to State Highway 183 and go north to Lockhart for a visit to the town hall, which sits on a site once occupied by the home of Alamo survivor Susanna Dickinson *(pages 4-6)*. From Lockhart, take State Highway 142 west to State Highway 80, then go north to Interstate 35 and continue north to Kyle for a visit to the Katherine Anne Porter Literary Center *(page 79)*. From Kyle, take FM 3237 west to Wimberly, then FM 2325 west to Blanco, stopping for lunch along the way. From Blanco, head north on U.S. Highway 281 to Johnson City. Spend the night there, or in the nearby German community of Fredericksburg. The following day, tour the Lyndon B. Johnson National Historical Park in Johnson City to get acquainted with the legacy of Lady Bird Johnson *(page 133)*. Return to San Antonio via U.S. Highway 281 South. To make this trip from Austin, leave the state capital heading south on U.S. Highway 183 and return from Johnson City via U.S. Highway 290. [2 to 3 days]

☙ Add a day to the preceding trip by adding two downtown San Antonio sites: the Alamo *(page 2)* and the Hertzberg Circus Museum *(page 33)*. [3 to 4 days]

☙ Expand the preceding two trips by one to three days by adding any of the Austin day trips to your itinerary. [3 to 7 days]

West Texas

☙ From Fort Worth, which touts itself as "where the West begins," head west on U.S. Highway 180 to Albany and visit the Sally Reynolds Matthews Room at the Old Jail Art Center *(page 85)*. From Albany, take U.S. Highway 283 south to Interstate 20 and head west through Abilene (skip the Abilene Mrs Baird's plant in favor of the Fort Worth site) then stop in Merkel to visit the site where World War II-era pilot Cornelia Fort died in a plane crash *(page 178)*. Backtrack to the interstate and continue west to Sweetwater. Plan to stay overnight in Sweetwater. While there, visit the town's Women Airforce Service Pilots sites. Be sure to make motel reservations if you plan to visit during the annual Rattlesnake Roundup. At other times of the year rooms are easy to come by. Return to Fort Worth the following day via Interstate 20 and round out your vacation by adding one of the Fort Worth day trips. [2 days]

❦ Expand the preceding trip by taking Interstate 20 west out of Sweetwater to Midland for a visit to the very cool American Heritage Airpower Museum *(page 180)*. Then take State Highway 158 east to U.S. Highway 87 and head south to San Angelo where a visit to Miss Hattie's Bordello Museum is not to be missed *(page 203)*. Spend the night in San Angelo, then take U.S. Highway 67 north to Brownwood for a visit to the grave of writer Katherine Anne Porter *(page 81)*. Then continue north on U.S. Highway 67, which turns into U.S. Highway 377 and return to Fort Worth. [4 to 5 days]

❦ This itinerary is a great add-on to a trip to Big Bend National Park. Head west on Interstate 10 to Fort Stockton (or take Interstate 20 west to Monahans, then go south on State Highway 18 to Fort Stockton.) Visit the Annie Riggs Memorial Museum *(page 140)*. Tour the rest of the town's historic sites and spend the night in Fort Stockton, or head south on U.S. Highway 385 toward Big Bend, stopping at Hallie's Hall of Fame Museum along the way *(page 72)*. Marathon, Big Bend, and Alpine are good places to spend a night or two ... or more. If you stay in Alpine, treat yourself to a meal at Reata. [2 to 5 days]

The Panhandle

❧ This trip is based in Amarillo. From there, head north to Cal Farley's Boys Ranch to immerse yourself in the romantic legend of Frenchy McCormick *(page 57)*. This will take at least half a day. After lunch in Amarillo, make a quick stop at the Amarillo Museum of Art to see its three Georgia O'Keeffe watercolors *(page 106)*, then head south on Interstate 27 to Canyon. Plan to spend the night in Canyon. The next day, tour the town's Georgia O'Keeffe sites *(pages 104-106)* then head to glorious Palo Duro Canyon, which sparked the artist's love affair with the Southwest. Spend a second night in Canyon, or return to Amarillo. [2 to 3 days]

❧ Expand the preceding itinerary by a day with a trip to Lubbock's Mrs Baird's plant *(page 29)*. Take Interstate 27 south from Amarillo to Lubbock. [3 to 4 days]

Index

A

Abilene, 29
Addison, 25
Alamo, 2-20
Albany, 85-86
Allen, Dr. Frances "Daisy," 117-119
Alpine, 73
Alsbury, Horace, 17
Alsbury, Juana Navarro, 16
Amarillo Museum of Art, 106
Amarillo, 57, 106-107
American Heritage Airpower Museum, 180
Ames, Harriet Potter, 21
Annie Riggs Memorial Museum, 140
Ash, Mary Kay, 25
Atlanta, 166
Austin, 5, 11, 37, 19, 50, 101, 113, 131, 134
Avenger Field, 174, 180

B

B-29 Superfortress, 182
Babe Didrikson Zaharias Museum and Visitor Center, 124
"Babe of the Alamo," 6-7, 9
Bailey, Blackie Hardesty, 36
Bailey, Gus, 34, 36
Bailey, Mollie, 33
Baird, Nina "Ninnie," 28, 30
Baird, William, 30

Bayou Bend, 111, 113
Beaumont, 124, 126
Bell County Museum, 39, 143
Bellis, Peter, 8
Belton, 143, 145
Belton Woman's Commonwealth, 143
bird migrations, 63
Blagg-Huey Library, 208
Blanton, Annie Webb, 37, 50-51
Bolivar Peninsula, 158
Bonner-Whitaker-McClendon House, 83
Bowie, James, 17
Brownwood, 81
Buffalo Bayou, 8

C

Cal Farley's Boys Ranch, 57
Canyon, 104-107
Carroll, Georgia, 211
Casimero Romero Cemetery, 58
Chamberlain Cemetery, 154
chili cook-off, 75
cholera epidemic, 17
City-County Pioneer Museum, 177
Civil War, 156
Cochran, Jacqueline, 180
Coleman, Bessie, 166-170
Collins, Eileen, 200-202
Columbus, 77
Columbus City Cemetery, 78

Connie Hagar Cottage
Sanctuary, 63
Connie Hagar Wildlife
Sanctuary, 62
Corpus Christi, 94-97
Corpus Christi-Days Inn
Airport, 97
Cowgirl Hall of Fame, 76
Crown Hill Memorial Park, 161
Cunningham, Minnie Fisher,
37, 41-42

D
Dallas, 160-161, 164, 179, 207,
211
DAR Museum, 210
Daughters and Sons of the
Heroes and Pioneers of the
Republic of Texas, 14
Daughters of the Republic of
Texas, 2, 11-12
Daughters of the Republic of
Texas Library, 4
Davis, Gussie Nell, 52-54
De Salinas, Victoriana, 20
De Zavala, Adina, 11
Democratic Party, 15, 45, 47,
49
Denton, 178, 208
Diamond Besse murder trial,
188
Dickinson, Almeron, 6-7
Dickinson, Angelina, 7-8
Dickinson, Susanna (*see*
Hannig, Susanna
Dickinson)
Dilue Rose Harris House
Museum, 77, 79
Driscoll, Clara, 4, 9, 11

E
East Columbia, 138
Elizabet Ney Museum, 101
Esparza, Ana Salazar, 15
Esparza, Enrique, 16, 20
Esparza, Gregorio, 15
Esparza, Maria de Jesus Castro,
15
Excelsior House Hotel, 186,
187

F
Fair Park, 207, 211
Farmersville Cemetery, 56
Federation Aeronautique
Internationale, 168
Ferguson, James Edward "Pa,"
40
Ferguson, Miriam "Ma," 37
Fifinella, 176, 177
First Ladies' dresses, 210
Forest Lawn Memorial Park,
126
Fort Stockton, 140
Fort Worth Medical College,
117-118
Fort Worth, 28, 115, 117, 206
Fort, Cornelia, 178
Frontiers of Flight Museum,
179

G
Galveston, 9, 42, 88, 129, 166
Gonzales, Petra, 16
Governor Hogg Shrine State
Historical Park, 109, 114
Grapevine, 161
Griffith, John Maynard, 8
Groesbeck, 148

H
Hagar, Connie, 62, 65
Hallett, John, 67-68, 70
Hallett, John Jr., 69-70
Hallett, Margaret, 67-68
Hallettsville, 67, 70
Hallettsville Garden and
    Cultural Center, 67
Hallie's Hall of Fame Museum,
    72, 76
Hannig, Susanna Dickinson,
    4-9, 19
Harris, Dilue Rose, 77
Hempstead, 101-102
Herndon, Dealey, 37
Hertzberg Circus Museum, 33
Hickenlooper, Lucy Jane Olga,
    88
Hogg, Ima, 109-114
Hoke, Douglas & Margaret,
    109
Hood's Texas Brigade, 34
Houston, 7-8, 47, 111-112, 113,
    169, 180, 192
Houston, Sam, 7, 122, 148
Houston Symphony Orchestra,
    113
Howard Hughes Field, 180
Hudspeth House, 105

I
Ima Hogg Museum, 114
Indian Creek Cemetery, 81
*Interwoven: A Pioneer
    Chronicle*, 86
itineraries, 213

J
Jacket, Barbara, 204
Jefferson, 21, 186-191

Jefferson Historical Pilgrimage,
    186
Jemison, Mae, 194-196
Jesse Allen Wise Garden Club,
    186-187
Johnson City, 133, 134
Johnson Space Center, 192
Johnson, Claudia Alta Taylor
    "Lady Bird," 131-137, 187
Johnson, Lyndon Baines, 45,
    49, 85, 135
Joplin, Janis, 91-94
Jordan, Barbara, 37, 47-49
    archives, 47

K
Karnack, 134
Katherine Anne Porter Literary
    Center, 79
Kellogg, Elizabeth, 148
Kemp, 160
Kemp Calaboose, 160, 161
Keyes, Evelyn, 204-205
Kilgore, 52
Kilgore College Rangerettes,
    52-53
King, Henrietta, 154-156, 206
King, Richard, 155
King Ranch, 154
Kingsville, 154, 156
Kyle, 80-81

L
La Porte, 120
Lady Bird Johnson Wildflower
    Center, 131
Lafitte, Jean, 158
Laguna Gloria, 9
Lavaca Historical Museum, 67
LBJ Ranch, 133

LBJ State Historical Park,
    133-134
Liendo Plantation, 101, 104
Lockhart, 4
Lone Star Flight Museum, 166
Long Barracks Museum, 3
Long, Jane Wilkinson, 157-159
Losoya, Concepcion, 19
Lucid, Shannon, 198-199
Lyndon Baines Johnson Library
    and Museum, First Lady's
    Gallery, 134
Lyndon B. Johnson National
    Historical Park, 133

M
Mann, Pamelia, 8
Mansion House Hotel, 8
Marathon, 75
Mary Kay Museum, 25
Matthews, Sallie Reynolds, 77,
    85-86
Mayfield, Sophia, 22, 24
McClendon, Sarah, 77, 83-85
McCormick, Elizabeth McGraw
    "Frenchy," 57-58
McCormick, Mickey "Mack,"
    58, 60
McWhirter, Martha White,
    143-147
Melton, Eliel, 19
Melton, Juana Francisca, 19
Memorial Coliseum, 95
Memorial Park Cemetery, 68
Merkel, 178
Midland, 180
Mineola, 109, 112
Mirdor del Flor, 95
Miss Hattie's Bordello
    Museum, 203

Molina neighborhood, 94-95
Moore, "Diamond" Bessie,
    189-191
Moorman, Dorothea "Doro"
    Johnson, 181-182
Morgan, Emily, 121
Morton Cemetery, 157
"Mother Hallett," 71
"Mother of Texas," 158
Museum of Science and
    History, 115
Museum of the Gulf Coast, 91,
    124, 204-205

N
Nation, Carry, 138-139
National Audubon Society, 66
National Cowgirl Hall of Fame,
    206
National League of Women
    Voters, 44
Navarro, Gertrudis, 16
Ney, Elizabet, 101-105
Nichols, Nichelle, 196
Ninety-Nines, 174

O
Oakwood Cemetery, Austin, 6,
    50, 112, 114
Oakwood Cemetery, Jefferson,
    191
Ochoa, Ellen, 196-198
O'Keeffe, Georgia, 104-108
Old Courthouse Museum, 57
Old Fort Parker Historical
    Park, 148-149
Old Jail Art Center, 85
Owen, Dr. May, 115

P
Palo Duro Canyon, 106

Panhandle Plains Museum, 104
Pappagallo, 97
Parker, Bonnie, 160-165
Parker, Cynthia Ann, 148-153
Parker, Topsannah, 152
Perez, Selena Quintanilla, 88, 94-100
Plummer, Rachel Parker, 148-150
Port Arthur, 91, 124,126, 204-205
Porter, Callie Russell, 81
Porter, Katherine Anne, 77, 79
Potter, Harriet (*see* Ames, Harriet Potter)
Potter, Robert, 22
Potter's Point, 21
Presidio, 73, 75
Pulitzer Prize, 82

Q
Quitman, 109, 114

R
Rangerette Showcase and Museum, 51
Rawls, Betsy, 129-130
Richmond, 157
Ride, Sally, 193
Riggs, Annie, 140-142
Rockport Cemetery, 63
Rockport, 62-64
Roosevelt, Eleanor, 208
Roosevelt, Franklin Delano, 45
Ross, Nellie, 40

S
Samaroff, Olga, 88-90
San Angelo, 203
San Antonio, 4, 33, 170, 174

San Jacinto Monument and Museum, 120
Sanctificationists, 143, 146-147
Santa Anna, 16, 19, 120-121
"Savior of the Alamo," 14
Seaside Memorial Cemetery, 97
Selena (*see* Perez, Selena Quintanilla)
Selena Museum, 94-95
Selena, Etc. boutique, 95, 97
Sevier, Henry Hulme, 14
Ship of Fools, 82
Shirley House, 105
Space Center Houston, 192
Space Shuttle *Atlantis*, 198
Space Shuttle *Challenger*, 193-194
Space Shuttle *Columbia*, 201
Space Shuttle *Discovery*, 199
Space Shuttle *Endeavor*, 194
Spring, 129
Stieglitz, Alfred, 107
Stillwell, Hallie, 72, 206
Stinson Aviation Company, 171
Stinson Field, 174
Stinson Sisters, 170-174
Stinson, Katherine, 166, 171-174
Stinson, Marjorie, 166, 171-174
Strother, Dora, 181-182
Sweetwater, 174, 176-178, 180

T
Tadlock, Thelma "Tad," 205
Tascosa, 58, 60
Tereshkova, Valentina, 193
Texas Air Museum, 170
Texas Black Woman's Archives, 207

Texas Christian University, 116
Texas Golf Hall of Fame, 129
Texas Historical Landmarks Society, 14
Texas Medical Association, 117
Texas Revolution, 78, 121
Texas Southern University, 47
Texas State Capitol Building, 37, 101
Texas State Cemetery, 39, 47
Texas White House, 133
Texas Woman's University, 54, 178, 208-210
The Collected Stories of Katherine Anne Porter, 82
"The Flying Schoolgirl," 171
The Women's Museum: An Institute for the Future, 37, 211-212
Threadgill, Kenneth, 94
Travis, William, 6
Tyler, 83-84

U
University of Texas, 51, 113, 114
University of Texas Medical Branch, 42, 44

V
Varner-Hogg Plantation State Historical Park, 110, 113

Veramendi, Ursula, 17

W
Waco, 30
WAFS (*see* Women's Auxiliary Ferrying Squadron)
WASP (*see* Women Airforce Service Pilots)
Watergate, 49
West Columbia, 110
West Oso Junior High School, 95
West, Emily, 122
A White House Diary, 137
Williams, John, 7
Wishing Well, 175-177
Woman's Christian Temperance Union, 139
Women Airforce Service Pilots, 166, 174-184
Women's Auxiliary Ferrying Squadron, 178, 180
World War I, 174
World War II, 84, 135, 180

Y
Yellow Rose of Texas, 120-123

Z
Zaharias, Babe Didrikson, 124-129

Photo Index

Alamo, The, 3
Annie Riggs, 141
Avenger Field today, 176
Babe Didrikson Zaharias Monument and Museum, 125
Babe Didrikson Zaharias, 128
Barbara Jordan, 48
Bessie Coleman, 169
Blagg-Huey Library at Texas Woman's University, 209
Bonner-Whitaker-McClendon House, 83
Bonnie Parker, 163
Claudia Alta "Lady Bird" Johnson, age 3, 132
Connie Hagar Cottage Sanctuary, 64
Connie Hagar Wildlife Sanctuary, 63
Cynthia Ann Parker and Topsannah, 151
De Zavala, Adina, 12
Diamond Bessie's grave, 191
The Dilue Rose Harris House Museum, 78
Douglas and Margaret Hoke at Ima Hogg's Birthplace, 110
Driscoll, Clara, 10
Eileen Collins, 201
Elizabet Ney, 103
Elizabeth McGraw "Frenchy" McCormick, 59

Ellen Ochoa, 197
Excelsior House Hotel, 187
Grave of Margaret Hallett, 69
Graves of Mack and Frenchy McCormick, 61
Gussie Nell Davis, 55
Hallie Stillwell, 74
Hallie's Hall of Fame Museum, 73
Hannig, Susanna Dickinson, 5
Harriet Potter Ames Monument, 23
Henrietta King, 155
Janis Joplin as a young musician, 92
Janis Joplin at the height of her success, 93
Katherine Anne Porter Literary Center, 80
Katherine Stinson, the Flying Schoolgirl, 172
Kemp Calaboose, 161
Lady Bird Johnson in Washington, D.C., 136
LBJ with the Kilgore College Rangerettes, 54
Mae Jemison, 195
Marjorie Stinson becomes an airmail pilot, 173
Martha White McWhirter, 145
Martha White McWhirter's home in Belton, 144
Mary Kay Ash, 27

Minnie Fisher Cunningham's bungalow, 43
Minnie Fisher Cunningham's campaign poster, 46
Mirador del Flor, 96
Miriam Ferguson taking the oath of office, 41
Mollie Bailey, 35
Nina "Ninnie" Baird, 31
Olga Samaroff, 89
Sally Reynolds Matthews, 87
Sally Ride, 193
San Jacinto Monument, 121
Selena, 99
Texas State Capitol Building, 38
Varner-Hogg Plantation Manor, 111
WASP Commander Jacqueline Cochran, 183
WASP trainees dunking a pal in the wishing well, 175
wishing well today, 177
Women's Museum, The: An Institute for the Future, 212